A 30-DA

ENTRuSTED

OVERCOMING THE INNER BATTLES OF STEWARDSHIP AND CALLING

JENNIFER MARRUFO

Entrusted: Overcoming the Inner Battles of Stewardship and Calling

Copyright © 2026 by Jennifer Marrufo

All rights reserved. No part of this publication may be reproduced, stored in a retrieval system, distributed or transmitted in any form or by any means—electronic, mechanical, photocopy, recording, or otherwise—without prior written permission from the publisher, except in the case of brief quotations embodied in critical articles or reviews and certain other noncommercial uses permitted by copyright law.

Published by Rewritten House, Carthage, Missouri

Unless otherwise noted, Scripture quotations are from the Holy Bible, New International Version®, NIV®. Copyright © 1973, 1978, 1984, 2011 by Biblica, Inc.® Used by permission of Zondervan. All rights reserved worldwide. The "NIV" and "New International Version" are trademarks registered in the United States Patent and Trademark Office by Biblica, Inc.

Scripture quotations marked AMP are from the Amplified® Bible. Copyright © 1954, 1958, 1962, 1964, 1965, 1987 by The Lockman Foundation. Used by permission. www.Lockman.org

Scripture quotations marked MSG are from The Message. Copyright © by Eugene H. Peterson 1993, 1994, 1995, 1996, 2000, 2001, 2002. Used by permission of NavPress. All rights reserved. Represented by Tyndale House Publishers, Inc.

Scripture quotations marked NLT are from the Holy Bible, New Living Translation. Copyright © 1996, 2004, 2007, 2013, 2015, 2017 by Tyndale House Foundation. Used by permission of Tyndale House Publishers, Inc., Carol Stream, Illinois 60188. All rights reserved.

ISBN 979-8-9996038-1-4 (paperback)

Acknowledgements

To my husband—thank you for every minute you held down the fort, wrangled the chaos, and gave me the space to chase down the words on these pages. You push me to become the woman God has called me to be. Your quiet support, wisdom, and steady presence made this possible more than you know.

To my children, Owen and Millie—you are the heartbeat behind every hard thing I do. You inspire me to rise, to stretch, to keep becoming. This is for you. May you always know that it's worth it to lean in, do the hard things, and follow Jesus wherever He leads. The fruit is coming.

To my circle of trusted readers and encouragers—Laurie, Kent, Chris, Cindy, Charlie, Anya, Ashley, Jeannie, and Audrey—thank you for every read, every note of encouragement, every time you stopped to say, "Keep writing." Your belief in me helped me believe in myself. With every kind word you reminded me why this matters.

To my sweet momma in Heaven—thank you for pushing me to do hard things, for nudging me out of my comfort zone, and for always teaching me to finish what I start. Thank you for every notebook, every pencil, and every quiet act of belief in me. I know you'd be so proud.

To Jesus—the One who truly shaped this message and this book, who continues to stir new passions within me, and who reminds me again and again that obedience is never wasted—this is for Your glory alone. There is nothing new under the sun, but there is always something sacred when we walk in step with You.

TABLE OF CONTENTS

07	INTRODUCTION
09	A CALL TO STEWARDSHIP
15	PERFECTIONISM
21	FROM COMPARISON TO CELEBRATION
25	GOD'S WAITING ROOM
29	INTENTIONAL YES, SACRED NO
33	TUNING IN
39	YOUR WORK IS NOT YOUR WORTH
43	REFILLED
47	CHOOSING GOD OVER APPROVAL
51	CALLED TO HIS PURPOSE, NOT OUR PLATFORM
57	COURAGE OVER CONFIDENCE
61	THE POWER OF YOUR WORDS
65	TRUSTING BEYOND YOUR COMFORT ZONE
69	FROM HUSTLE TO HOLY REST
75	NAYSAYERS
79	CO-CREATOR

83	MARKETPLACE MINISTRY
87	GOD OF ORDER
91	A JAR OF OIL
95	OVERCOMING FEAR
99	SUCCESS IS OBEDIENCE
103	FREE FROM YESTERDAY
109	INDECISION
113	WHEN PRESSURE BRINGS PURPOSE
117	NO HOLINESS IN STRUGGLE
123	HEDGE OF PROTECTION
121	SACRED SEPARATION
125	UNSETTLED BUT LED
133	FROM SCARCITY TO ABUNDANCE
137	ENLARGE MY TERRITORY
143	NOTES
144	AUTHOR BIO
146	A PERSONAL INVITATION

INTRODUCTION

You feel it, don't you?

That persistent stirring. That quiet nudge that won't go away. It's a sense that you were made for more than the daily grind. Whether it's a business idea you've hesitated to seize, a ministry opportunity you've tucked away, or a drive to lead with Kingdom values in a marketplace that often ignores them—it refuses to leave you alone.

To every leader, creative, entrepreneur, and hardworking professional holding this book in their hands—I see you.

For too long, we have believed the lie that ministry only happens inside the church, while everything else is simply a means to pay the bills. Maybe you've suppressed something God placed on your heart be-cause you believed the lie that you have to stay small and do quiet work. Or maybe you've questioned if God could truly use someone like you—with your messy past, your current limitations, or your quiet fears.

But hear this: God never intended for a wall to exist between your Sunday faith and your Monday work.

Whether you are in the boardroom, in the studio, or a job site, the work of your hands is a divine opportunity for worship. God didn't place you in this world to only pass through it. He designed you to make a difference. And the gifts He's placed in your hands—your time, children, talent, vision, resources, and influence—are not random. They have been *entrusted* to you.

Still, the journey isn't easy. Sometimes it's lonely. Sometimes the road ahead is blurry. Comparison often shouts louder than faith. Obedience comes with no applause. And the work we are called to doesn't always look impressive. But if you've ever longed to make something meaningful—to pour your heart into your gifts and use them in a way that glorifies God—yet wrestled with the fear that you're too late, too broken, or too uncertain, this devotional is for you.

I know this battle well.

I'm no theologian writing from a mountaintop; this is an offering from the trenches. It comes from places where I doubted my value, questioned my voice, and almost let fear silence me. Where surrender felt like weakness—until I discovered it was the strongest move I could make.

I know what it's like to wrestle between dreaming big and staying grounded in truth. But that is exactly where God met me.

It's where His truth began to redefine how I saw my work, my gifts, my identity, and my assignment.

This book is the result.

It is a collection of what has carried me and what has transformed me. These 30 devotions serve as a field guide to help you overcome the inner battles of stewardship and calling. They will walk with you through the paralyzing fear of failure and the quiet compromise of settling for comfort, pointing you back to the One who called you in the first place.

This is your invitation to bridge the gap between "sacred" calling and "secular" work. It is a call into holy labor—partnering with God to turn your creativity into worship, your work into witness, and your process into praise.

Because God isn't asking for perfection.

He's asking for participation.

So let this book be a crucial reminder: You are not behind. You are not forgotten. You are not disqualified. God is with you in every season. He sees you when the doors stay closed, when inspiration wanes, and when the resistance feels heavy. And He is faithful to fill your hands with strength, courage, and fresh vision.

The world needs the fullness of what He's given you. Your leadership, your ideas, your service, your art, your story—they aren't just for you. They are a means to draw others to the goodness and greatness of our God and His Kingdom.

So let's step forward together—not in our own strength, but trusting that our God-given gifts are sacred and needed to shine His light into the dark places.

Let's use our gifts for His glory, knowing that our offerings are holy—no matter the size.

Let's trust with hearts fully open and hands willing, that even ordinary obedience ripples with Kingdom impact.

You've been gifted intentionally. Crafted uniquely. Called purposefully.

There is work only you can do.

For His Kingdom.

For His glory.

With our whole selves, let's embrace this journey together.

With hope for all you are becoming,

Jen

DAY ONE

A CALL TO STEWARDSHIP

SCRIPTURE: MATTHEW 25:14-30

Imagine being one of the servants in this story. The Master calls you over, places something of great value in your hands, looks you in the eye, and says, *"I trust you with this. Manage it while I'm away."* What would you do next? Would you deploy the resources with confidence, or would fear creep in, convincing you to play it safe?

So often, we wrestle with doubts, questioning whether we have enough resources or if we *are* enough for the task. But God has placed something in each of our hands—not by accident, but with purpose. And how we respond reveals not only our faith but our under-standing of who God is and what He's called us to do.

THE MASTER'S TRUST: WHAT HAS GOD PLACED IN YOUR HANDS?

It's important to note that in Jesus' day, a *talent* wasn't skills or abilities—it was a large sum of money. Over time, it has come to symbolize anything God has entrusted to us—our time, gifts, abilities, resources, and influence. And in this Scripture, Jesus is making it clear: *what we do with what we've been given matters.*

> *"Again, it will be like a man going on a journey, who called his servants and entrusted his wealth to them. To one he gave five bags of gold, to another two bags, and to another one bag, each according to his ability. Then he went on his journey." (vs. 14-15)*

We meet a Master who departs on a journey, leaving his servants with talents and clear expectations for their productivity and stewardship in his absence. This message resonates with believers today, offering instruction as we also await our Lord's return.

Think of it like this: if your life were a business, your gifts would be the capital. And God? He's the investor, expecting a return. Not because He needs anything from us, but because He desires us to participate in the growth of His Kingdom.

Scripture tells us the Master entrusted *his* property to his servants. That means everything we have ultimately belongs to God. He's the Owner; we are the asset managers. He also knows your capacity. He gives *"each according to his ability."* Not according to what looks fair or equal. The assignment may not match what someone else has, but it's been measured out with divine wisdom tailored to your specific ability to manage it.

FAITHFULNESS OVER FEAR: THE SERVANTS' RESPONSES

> *"The man who had received five bags of gold went at once and put his money to work and gained five bags more. So also, the one with two bags of gold gained two more. But the man who had received one bag went off, dug a hole in the ground, and hid his master's money." (vs. 16-18)*

The first two servants didn't hesitate. They took what they were given and put it to work. But the third servant buried his bag in fear.

When we focus on what we lack or what we stand to lose, fear is quick to take root and keep us from stepping into God's plan.

This passage also warns us against the trap of comparison, which loves to whisper lies that we deserve more. Like the third servant, seeing others receive more than us might stir up questions. We may look at someone else's talents or opportunities and wonder, *Why them and not me?*

But if you notice, the focus of this parable isn't on the amount given, but on the response of each servant.

God never asks us to steward what someone else has been given—only what we have been given. Faithfulness isn't about having *much*—it's about *trusting* much and doing much with what you have been entrusted.

THE REWARD OF FAITHFUL STEWARDSHIP

> *"After a long time, the master of those servants returned and settled accounts with them. The man who had received five bags of gold brought the other five. 'Master,' he said, 'you entrusted me with five bags of gold. See, I have gained five more.'*
>
> *His master replied, 'Well done, good and faithful servant! You have been faithful with a few things; I will put you in charge of many things. Come and share your master's happiness!'*
>
> *The man with two bags of gold also came. 'Master,' he said, 'you entrusted me with two bags of gold; see, I have gained two more.'*
>
> *His master replied, 'Well done, good and faithful servant! You have been faithful with a few things; I will put you in charge of many things. Come and share your master's happiness!'" (vs. 19-23)*

When the Master returned to settle accounts, the servants who doubled their investment (each starting with two different amounts) received the exact same praise:

"Well done, good and faithful servant."

Notice the metric. Not, *"Well done, successful servant,"* or *"Well done, famous servant."* He said, *Faithful.*

Jesus' words show that faithfulness—not the scale of the return—is what pleases God. The servant with two talents was not compared to the one with five; both were commended equally.

Success in God's economy is obedience. He calls us to obedience—not to results our of our control.

Then we meet the third servant.

THE DANGER OF PLAYING IT SAFE

> *"Then the man who had received one bag of gold came. 'Master,' he said, 'I knew that you are a hard man, harvesting where you have not sown and gathering where you have not scattered seed. So I was afraid and went out and hid your gold in the ground. See, here is what belongs to you.'"* (vs. 24-25)

Notice his view of the Master. Instead of seeing him as generous and trusting—giving him an opportunity to steward and build—this servant saw him as "a hard man." Projecting his own failings onto the Master, he saw him as demanding and unreasonable. His perception of the Master was skewed, and that belief, along with his self-centeredness, shaped his strategy.

He failed—not because he wasn't capable, or wasn't given enough, but because he acted out of fear rather than reverence, which led to inaction. Instead of investing, he hoarded. Instead of trusting, he retreated.

How often do we do the same? How often do we let fear convince us to play it safe—to "hold the line" rather than advance? To hide the very gifts God has called us to leverage for the Kingdom?

Fear reveals the characteristics of this servant: idle, unproductive, and focused on self-preservation rather than Kingdom impact. He refused to engage with the opportunity, ultimately prioritizing his own comfort over the Master's interests.

Understanding God as generous, just, and trustworthy compels us to act in faith. This servant wasn't condemned because he had less—he was condemned because he refused to act. We are not owners of our gifts, time, money, resources, or influence. We are caretakers.

Sometimes, the greatest tragedy is not losing what we've been given—it's refusing to use it at all.

A CALL TO STEWARDSHIP

Sometimes, the greatest tragedy is not losing what we've been given—it's refusing to use it at all.

Unfaithful stewardship has consequences. While our salvation is by grace through faith *(Ephesians 2:8-9)*, our stewardship in serving God matters and will be accounted for. We are not saved by works, but we do have a choice: to live for ourselves, or to invest our lives for God's glory.

Jesus Himself modeled this perfection. He used what was given to Him, according to His ability, trusted the Father, and invested His life for our benefit.

Just as the Master in the parable returns to settle accounts, our Lord will return. We, too, will give an account for how we stewarded everything He entrusted to us.

Let us embrace the opportunities before us to steward our gifts well, taking calculated risks in faith, and acting with the confidence that our Lord is returning.

May we live in such a way that when we stand before Him, we hear the only performance review that matters: *"Well done, good and faithful servant."*

PRAYER:

Father, thank You for entrusting me with this life, these gifts, and these opportunities. Help me to stop striving for what I don't have and instead be faithful with what You've already given me. Keep me from fear, comparison, and risk-aversion. Remind me that success in Your eyes is about faithfulness. Give me the courage to step out, invest my talents, and trust You with the results. I want to serve you well. In Jesus' name, Amen.

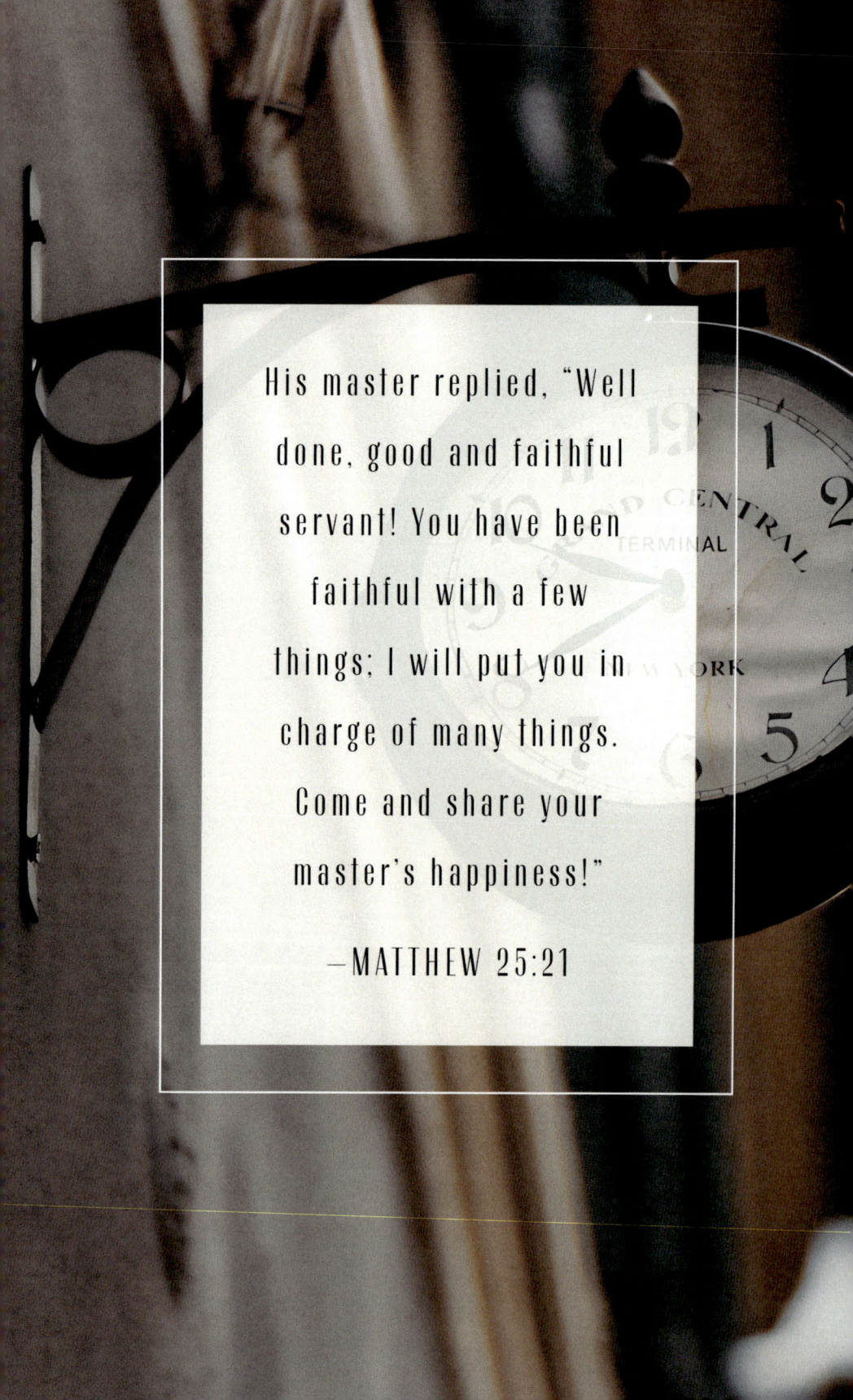

His master replied, "Well done, good and faithful servant! You have been faithful with a few things; I will put you in charge of many things. Come and share your master's happiness!"

—MATTHEW 25:21

DAY TWO

PERFECTIONISM

> **SCRIPTURE:**
>
> *He who watches the wind [waiting for all conditions to be perfect] will not sow [seed], and he who looks at the clouds will not reap [a harvest].* —Ecclesiastes 11:4 AMP

Have you ever felt stuck by the fear of not getting something *just right*? We long to offer our best, but too often, in our pursuit, we find ourselves frozen in place. Our creative ideas stay in the notebook. The project remains unfinished. The dream sits in the planning stage.

Why? Because we're waiting—maybe for the perfect timing, when life feels a little less chaotic. Waiting until we have the perfect plan so we can 'do it justice'. Waiting for the perfect outcome because, let's be honest, our reputation is on the line. But if we wait for everything to be perfect, we may never start. Or, if we do start, we may never finish.

Our Scripture today paints a vivid picture of this struggle. Imagine a farmer standing in his field, watching the sky, waiting for the perfect conditions before planting. But as he waits on the wind, the season slips by, and his field remains empty.

Perfectionism can do the same thing to our creative work. If we wait until every variable is controlled, our ideas and potential may go unsown.

I know this struggle well. I've doubted my abilities and prolonged projects countless times because I feared the result wouldn't be *good enough*. But my thinking was rooted in fear—that my gifts wouldn't measure up to the standards I set, that I wasn't qualified, or that my work wouldn't make the impact I desired. I constantly hid behind the label of "excellence" to justify the delay, when in reality, it was a mask for my inner doubts.

Perfectionism, though it can sometimes stem from a genuine desire to honor God, isn't typically a matter of pursuing excellence. It's more about trying to control every outcome.

We dress it up as high standards, but beneath that polished label lies a deep-seated need to hold on tightly—to orchestrate every detail. In reality, that drive is less about quality and more about concealing our fear and our reluctance to trust God with the unpredictable process of something new.

But God never asked us to be perfect.

He asks us to be *faithful*.

In *1 Timothy 4:15*, Paul encourages Timothy not to strive for perfection but to practice his gifts, to immerse himself in them, so that others would see his progress.

Did you catch that?

Not his *flawlessness*—His *progress*.

When we trust God with our gifts, we trade the weight of perfectionism for the freedom found in obedience. We surrender our need to control the results and instead step forward, believing that God will use our offering even in its imperfection.

When we trust God with our gifts, we trade the weight of perfectionism for the freedom found in obedience.

The apostle Paul reminds us that *"God's power is made perfect in our weakness"* (2 Corinthians 12:9). That means our perceived shortcomings don't disqualify us. Rather, they position us for His strength to shine through.

So, what if your work isn't about getting it all right, but about simply surrendering it to God?

What if the real breakthrough isn't in your execution, but accepting the assignment and trusting Him with the process?

What if the real breakthrough isn't in your execution, but accepting the assignment and trusting Him with the process?

PRACTICAL STEPS TO HELP OVERCOME PERFECTIONISM

Here are a few practical ways to recognize when your pursuit of excellence is tipping into perfectionism, and steps to help you overcome it:

1. EXAMINE YOUR MOTIVATION

Begin by examining your heart. Is your pursuit of excellence coming from a desire to glorify God? Or is it driven by a need to control the outcome, earn approval, or shield yourself from criticism? When your motivation is firmly rooted in worship and service, it creates space to trust that God can work through even what feels imperfect.

2. SET CLEAR BOUNDARIES & DEADLINES

Give yourself a hard stop. Decide in advance how much time you will devote to revisions or planning. This isn't about compromising quality; it's about freeing yourself from endless "what-ifs" so you can move forward. If we never plant the seeds of our work because we're too busy refining them, we deny them the chance to grow. Accept that sometimes the act of finishing is an act of faith.

*Sometimes the act of finishing
is an act of faith.*

3. EMBRACE "GOOD ENOUGH FOR NOW"

Find freedom in embracing the idea that good enough for now is better than perfect never. Recognize that your best effort is often enough to start. When you finish a task, pause and ask God to use it, imperfections and all. Trust that He can use what you offer to make an impact. Remember Paul's encouragement to Timothy—it's about *progress*.

Find freedom in embracing the idea that "good enough for now is better than perfect never."

At the end of the day, the line between excellence and perfectionism can be found in your motives. The goal is to develop a relationship with God in which you learn to trust His timing and perspective on your work.

Ask God to help you see that your faithful effort is enough—because He is the one who ultimately establishes our work.

When you're driven by the love of God and the desire to use your gifts for His glory, you can rest in the assurance that what you've done is enough—even if it's not flawless.

The world doesn't need more flawless efforts; it needs more surrendered ones. It needs us to make an offering, trusting that God will make it count.

PERFECTIONISM

*The world doesn't need more flawless efforts; it needs more **surrendered** ones.*

Proverbs 3:27 *(NLT)* reminds us to *"not withhold good from those who deserve it when it's in your power to help them."* While you wait to feel fully ready or for the perfect conditions, someone out there may be longing for the solution, encouragement, or leadership only you can offer.

In releasing our need for control and stepping forward in faith, we honor the Lord and become a blessing to others. Let's not allow our pursuit of perfection to mask our fear. Instead, let our willingness to share our progress speak louder than our hesitation.

PRAYER:

Lord, forgive me for my need to control every detail of my life and work. Help me embrace the freedom that comes from letting go of self-reliance. Teach me to see that my worth is found in You—not in flawless execution—but in my willingness to obey Your call. Thank You for revealing that Your plans for me don't hinge on my perfection, but on my obedience. Father, I believe in Your power and ability to create something unexpected and beautiful from my imperfect offering. In Jesus' name, Amen.

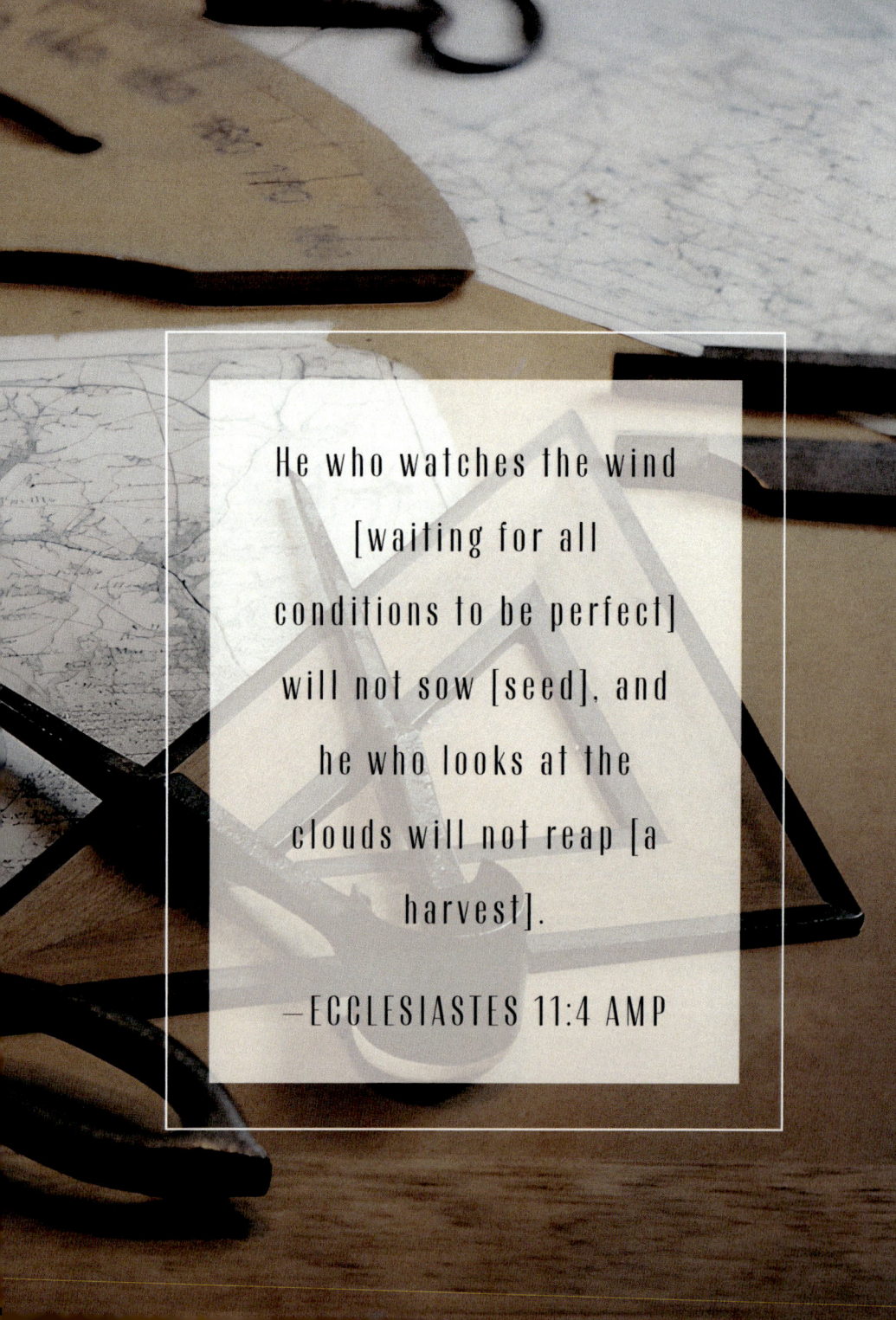

He who watches the wind [waiting for all conditions to be perfect] will not sow [seed], and he who looks at the clouds will not reap [a harvest].

—ECCLESIASTES 11:4 AMP

DAY THREE

FROM COMPARISON TO CELEBRATION

SCRIPTURE:

Each one should test their own actions. Then they can take pride in themselves alone, without comparing themselves to someone else. —Galatians 6:4

Ever catch yourself scrolling through social media, seeing peers seemingly thriving in their callings, executing their gifts so effortlessly, and thinking, *If only I could be where they are?*

It's easy to look at someone else's trajectory—their growing platform, their booming business, or their apparent impact—and assume their journey has been smoother or their purpose clearer. We reach a milestone, feeling good about our progress until we see someone else's "win", and suddenly, our own success seems to dim in their shadow.

We struggle to genuinely celebrate others' achievements because a quiet voice whispers, *They are already doing it—and doing it better.* And just like that, the joy is drained from the work God is doing in us.

Comparison is a thief.

It steals our gratitude and stalls our momentum.

Why do we allow someone else's purpose to make us feel less worthy of our own? When we feel triggered by comparison, it often means we're placing our worth on shaky ground—things like achievement, recognition, or others' approval. The moment we see someone else excelling in our lane, insecurity floods in, convincing us we don't measure up.

It's easy for everything we've been blessed with or accomplished to pale in the face of comparison.

The enemy uses these feelings to weaponize our own ambition against us. His goal is to plant a scarcity mindset—the lie that there's a limited amount of success available, that there's a shortage of Kingdom work, and that your God-given gifts are somehow redundant because someone else had them first.

But the truth is that God's economy isn't a zero-sum game! His plans for you are as uniquely designed as you are. And when He calls another leader to build, or another creative to design, it's not a subtraction from your calling—it's an addition to His Kingdom.

God's economy isn't a zero-sum game! His plans for you are as uniquely designed as you are. And when He calls another leader to build, or another creative to design, it's not a subtraction from your calling—it's an addition to His Kingdom.

Our verse today reminds us to pay close attention to our own work and focus on what God has placed in our hearts. You can't focus on your own assignment when you are too busy trying to insert yourself into someone else's story. We each have a specific field to tend, a unique team to lead, and a distinct purpose woven into the bigger plan for God's Kingdom.

Your specific role is essential. The gifts you hold—your artistic eye, your strategic mind, your ability to build culture—are irreplaceable because they are entrusted to you.

One antidote to comparison is celebration. So, the next time you're tempted to compare your "behind-the-scenes" with someone else's "highlight reel," try celebrating them instead. Let the success of a peer remind you of God's abundance, because when we celebrate others rather than compete with them, we break the cycle of scarcity thinking and usher in a spirit of Kingdom unity.

There's plenty of space for every steward to walk faithfully in their God-given purpose.

Secondly, when you catch yourself feeling discouraged or "less than" because of a competitor's success, take it to God immediately. Prayer is where comparison loses its power.

Ask Him to remind you that what He has planned for them doesn't take away from what He has planned for you. When you feel inadequate, surrender those thoughts—and then pray for the person who stirred them up. This shifts your heart from rivalry to humility. There's plenty of space for every steward to walk faithfully in their God-given purpose.

Prayer is where comparison loses its power.

While it's easy to compare the work you've poured your heart into with the perceived perfection you see in someone else's life, you don't know the depth of their journey or the cost they paid to get there.

You're seeing the fruit, not the fight.

Remember, while there may always be someone ahead of you, there is also someone right behind you, watching how you handle your own race.

Instead of fixating on what you lack or chasing someone else's purpose, wholeheartedly embrace your own. God's assignment for you is filled with depth and opportunity that are yours alone. His Kingdom isn't a race or a ladder; it's a place where we each have a unique and purposeful calling.

When we focus on our own God-given gifts and rejoice in the callings of others, we can fully enjoy the work He's given us. Let's use our gifts to build His Kingdom, staying confident in the truth that God's plans are abundant enough for everyone to fulfill their calling.

ENTRUSTED

PRAYER:

Father, You are the giver of every good gift, the author of every unique calling, and the Creator of endless opportunities to reflect Your glory. Yet so often, I lose sight of the work You're doing in me because I'm too busy looking at what You're doing in someone else. Help me shift my focus back to my own assignment. Teach me to celebrate the victories of others—not as a threat or measure of my worth, but as evidence of Your abundant goodness. Let their success inspire me to trust that there's no shortage in Your Kingdom, only an overflow of Your creativity and grace. In Jesus' name, Amen.

DAY FOUR

GOD'S WAITING ROOM

> ### SCRIPTURE:
>
> *But those who wait for the Lord [who expect, look for, and hope in Him] Will gain new strength and renew their power; They will lift up their wings [and rise up close to God] like eagles [rising toward the sun]; They will run and not become weary, They will walk and not grow tired.* —Isaiah 40:31 AMP

Have you ever sat in a waiting room, fidgeting in your chair, checking your watch, scanning the same magazine you've already flipped through five times? The fluorescent lights buzz overhead, and the air carries a strong scent of cheap coffee with a tinge of antiseptic. You keep glancing toward the receptionist, looking for a sign of movement, hoping your name will finally be called. But it isn't.

Waiting feels unproductive, frustrating, and, if we're honest, like a waste of our potential. You feel the urgency of the vision, the project, or the ministry idea laying dormant. The excitement you once felt is beginning to dull under the weight of time. Doubt starts to creep in, and you begin to wonder: *God, where are You?*

Did I miss the plan?

I know this feeling well. In fact, I see it every day in my son. When he's ready to go outside, there's an urgency. An undeniable spark. He's got big plans for that backyard—adventures to chase, mud to dig. But in the short time it takes to slip on his shoes, impatience sets in. The desire to move outpaces the readiness to sustain the moment. He's ready *now*.

And aren't we just like that with God? We want to rush out the door, but He knows we need to be equipped first.

The Bible is full of stories of people who had to wait before stepping into their assignments. Consider David. His journey from anointing to kingship spanned about 15 years—years filled with challenges that shaped him.

Chosen by God as the future king of Israel while he was still a shepherd boy, David didn't step into his position immediately. But he also didn't wait idly. He didn't sit on a rock wishing for the throne. In the waiting, I assume he fought battles, honed his skill with a sling, learned to lead men in the wilderness, and cultivated a heart after the Lord.

God used the waiting room to shape David into a man who could handle the weight of the crown.

What if your waiting season isn't a delay, but divine preparation?

What if your waiting season isn't a delay, but divine preparation?

In a culture of instant gratification, waiting is wasted time. It tells us if you aren't scaling, you're failing. But God sees things differently. While we wait, He is aligning circumstances, refining our character and strengthening our capacity to carry the calling He has given us.

While we wait, He is aligning circumstances, refining our character and strengthening our capacity to carry the calling He has given us.

In our verse today, we're told that those who *wait* for the Lord will gain new strength. The Hebrew word here for "*wait*" is *qavah*. It implies tension—like a rope stretched tight. It's potential energy building up, ready to be released. This waiting is not about being passive; it's about waiting with active expectation.

HEBREW: 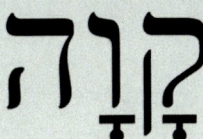 *Qavah* means to wait for, look eagerly, hope, or expect. It conveys an active, tension-filled waiting—like twisting cords together—signifying endurance, trust, and confident expectation in God's timing and faithfulness.[1]

Waiting on God isn't idle time. It's an active trust. We are stretching, preparing, and fully expecting that His faithfulness will unfold in ways we can't even imagine yet.

*Waiting on God isn't idle time.
It's an active trust.*

Think of an artist stepping back from her canvas. She isn't pausing because she's lost interest—she's gaining perspective. She's letting the paint settle, ensuring each brushstroke and color fits into the masterpiece she's creating.

Or consider an architect's grueling preparation before breaking ground. He is ensuring the foundation can hold the weight of the structure.

In the same way, God is cultivating something in you. The waiting isn't a sign of neglect—it's proof that He's making sure you're deeply rooted, ready to sustain the calling when the season changes.

If you're in God's waiting room regarding your career or next assignment, know this: He hasn't forgotten you.

He isn't ignoring your prayers. As you watch others move ahead, know that He is preparing you. And when the time is right—when your character matches your gifting—He will open the door.

Until then, keep showing up. Keep refining. Keep leading faithfully in the quiet. Because while you are waiting, He is working.

ENTRUSTED

PRAYER:

Father, I confess that waiting is hard. I want to move forward, but I trust that You are working in the unseen. Help me to embrace this season as preparation, not punishment. Strengthen my heart, deepen my faith, and align my desires with Your perfect will. Thank You for being a God who sees, who knows, and who is always faithful. In Jesus' name, Amen.

DAY FIVE

INTENTIONAL YES, SACRED NO

5

SCRIPTURE:

Therefore see that you walk carefully [living life with honor, purpose, and courage; shunning those who tolerate and enable evil], not as the unwise, but as wise [sensible, intelligent, discerning people], making the very most of your time [on earth, recognizing and taking advantage of each opportunity and using it with wisdom and diligence], because the days are [filled with] evil.
—Ephesians 5:15-16 AMP

Are you a chronic accommodator? The go-to person who takes on every request, no matter the cost?

Perhaps you agree because you don't want to let anyone down or miss a potential opportunity. And now, you've found yourself juggling it all—the PTA, serving in a new role at church, and the networking event—all while trying to show up for your family, lead your team, and grow your business.

Sometimes our "Yes" is healthy. Other times, it comes from a desire to please others or is rooted in pride—a quiet whisper saying, *"I should be able to handle this,"* or *"If I don't do it, it won't get done right."* But guilt and pride are terrible motivators, often pulling us into commitments that leave us drained and resentful.

When we aren't paying attention, we say yes on autopilot. It slips out before we've counted the cost. Then, as the deadline approaches, we wonder why we agreed in the first place.

When we don't feel the repercussions of a commitment right away, it's easy to convince ourselves it's no big deal—until it is.

Scripture reminds us: *"Each of you should give what you have decided in your heart to give, not reluctantly or under compulsion"*

(2 Corinthians 9:7). While we often apply this verse to finances, it speaks just as powerfully to how we steward our time and energy.

When our "Yes" comes from obligation rather than a willing heart, we're not truly giving—we're simply avoiding disappointment. That is not stewardship; it's self-preservation. It's like giving a begrudging offering, which ultimately doesn't serve anyone. That's not God's desire for us.

I used to believe that serving others meant saying yes to every request, as if that's what made me a "good Christian." So, if there was a need, I filled it. If someone asked, I agreed. But this lifestyle is unsustainable. Even Jesus did not meet every need presented to Him, but prioritized His mission. He withdrew to pray (Luke 5:15-16) and moved on when necessary, even when people continued to seek Him.

Saying yes to everything easily pulls us away from the very things God has specifically called us to. God didn't call us to be human *doings* but human *beings*. He desires a connection with us to whisper His purpose and direction into our hearts. But how can we hear Him when we're drowning in the noise of endless commitments?

God hasn't called you to fill every gap. In fact, He calls you to use your time strategically.

The Scripture today reminds us—we must be careful how we live. Our time is a precious commodity, a finite resource, a sacred gift from God, and we are responsible for how we invest it. As stewards of our time, we bear the responsibility to discern when to decline. Saying "No" isn't selfish; it's wise. It's the only way to protect the specific assignment God has placed on your life.

As stewards of our time, we bear the responsibility to discern when to decline.

What would it look like if we chose to reclaim intentional living? What if *"making the most of every opportunity"* meant discerning which opportunities are truly from God and which are distractions pulling us away from our core mission?

Every time we say yes to a peripheral project, we are saying no to something else—perhaps strategic planning, deep creative work, or quality time with our families. While our "Yes" is often given to good things, we simply must be wise about the trades we're making.

For some of us, it's not the big commitments that derail us but the small, seemingly harmless yeses that pile up and chip away at our capacity. It's the unnecessary meeting, the extra coffee date, the late-night scroll, or the *just one more episode* that turns into three. These choices erode our margin for what truly matters.

Sometimes, when the Lord nudges us, it's easier to claim we're "too busy" than to take an honest look at our priorities. But the time we need often exists—we just need to redirect it.

That alignment starts with discernment—asking God what He's calling us to pick up and what He's asking us to release. In that obedience, our "Yes" is given to the highest good.

Before agreeing to a new commitment, ask yourself: *Does this align with the gifts and assignment God has given me for this season? What am I prioritizing today, and what am I unintentionally sacrificing because of it?*

What am I prioritizing today, and what am I unintentionally sacrificing because of it?

When we live with wisdom and intentionality, guided by God's Spirit, we find freedom in knowing that "No" is a complete sentence. It doesn't require an apology or explanation. Instead, it creates space for the God-ordained best. In that space, we experience the joy and fulfillment that comes from aligning our lives with His purpose.

Let's stop measuring our worth by how many plates we can keep spinning. Instead, let's embrace the sacredness of saying "No" as a God-honoring response, ensuring we have the capacity to give our full "Yes" to the work He has actually called us to do.

ENTRUSTED

PRAYER:

Heavenly Father, help me recognize the moments where I need to say "No," so I can make room for the divine "Yes" You've planned for me. Give me the wisdom to discern where to pour out my gifts, my energy, and my time. Pour out Your wisdom to accept what truly reflects Your assignment for me. May I steward my gifts for Your glory, living out my purpose with joy, peace, and a heart fully surrendered to You. In Jesus' name, Amen.

DAY SIX

TUNING IN

6

> **SCRIPTURE:**
>
> *Do not quench [subdue, or be unresponsive to the working and guidance of] the [Holy] Spirit.* —1 Thessalonians 5:19 AMP

Have you ever found yourself searching for clarity, wishing for God to hand you a perfectly laid-out plan? The kind of roadmap where every milestone is marked, every risk is calculated, and the outcome is guaranteed?

You want divine confirmation to move forward with certainty. And if you're anything like me, you've spent countless hours trying to "figure it all out," striving to connect the dots of what God is calling you to do.

But what if God's direction isn't always about handing you a blueprint? What if it's about cultivating a relationship of trust—a daily choice to listen to His Spirit, even when the path feels uncertain?

In my own journey, I've discovered that, unfortunately, God rarely shouts His plans. Sometimes the next step isn't a profound revelation but a quiet invitation to lean on His presence and tune our ear to His voice.

We often miss it because we are looking for a billboard when God is offering a breath. We crave an 'ah-ha' moment of clarity, but He is offering the steady, quiet rhythm of His presence.

When we're willing to listen, He shows us that His direction doesn't always look like a perfect itinerary. Often, it's a daily reliance on His Spirit to guide each step, to breathe life into our gifts, and to remind us that His plans for us often go beyond what we can imagine.

Sometimes the next step isn't a profound revelation but a quiet invitation to something much deeper—to lean on His presence and tune our ear to His voice.

Discernment—the ability to sense God's direction in our lives—is one of the most critical assets we have as we navigate the complex balance of work, leadership, and calling.

Walking with God means not only hearing, but actively listening to His promptings—requiring us to be sensitive, aware, and responsive, without letting our own agendas drown out His voice.

Walking with God means not only hearing, but actively listening to His promptings—requiring us to be sensitive, aware, and responsive, without letting our own agendas drown out His voice.

Have you ever felt a nudge to do something—a quiet check in your spirit—only to brush it off as a fleeting thought?

Perhaps it was something small, like leaving a generous tip, or a weightier prompting to take a step of faith and speak the hard truth to someone. These aren't mere whims. While not every impulse is from God, these consistent promptings are often the Holy Spirit inviting us into deeper trust and obedience. When we ignore the Spirit's voice, we risk dulling our sensitivity to it, becoming less attuned to His direction over time.

In our Scripture today, we're instructed, *"Do not quench the Spirit."* Quenching the Spirit means repeatedly suppressing His influence—ignoring the "gut check" or the quiet instruction.

These small moments are as if God is saying, *Listen to Me—I am guiding you.*

At times, His voice is clear and direct, like His guidance in Isaiah 30:21: *"This is the way; walk in it."* Other times, He speaks with a quiet *"Not right now,"* urging us to release an opportunity we might otherwise fight to keep. By consistently responding to these small whispers, we train our hearts to hear Him more clearly for the big decisions.

When we ignore the Spirit's voice, we risk dulling our sensitivity to it, becoming less attuned to His direction over time.

Life's distractions are swift to drown out the inner awareness of God's voice. Things like busyness, validation, and the loud opinion of experts make it hard to discern what God is saying.

Think about it. How often have you overcomplicated a decision, letting the noise around you distract from His leading?

When we surrender and follow the Holy Spirit's guidance, we are invited into greater confidence and peace—an assurance that we're on the right path, even if it defies conventional wisdom.

Proverbs 1:5 (NIV) reminds us, *"Let the wise listen and add to their learning, and let the discerning get guidance."* Our human knowledge alone isn't enough. We need discernment to know how to apply it. Then, true wisdom comes as the fruit of walking in step with His Spirit.

PRACTICAL WAYS TO TUNE IN:

1. STUDY SCRIPTURE

God's direction always aligns with His Word. His promptings will be wrapped in Scripture and will never contradict His character. If anything requires compromising integrity, it isn't from Him.

2. PRAYER & SILENCE

Bring your plans to God in prayer, but don't just talk—listen. And more than once. Regular moments of silence create space for His voice to cut through the noise of the grind.

3. LOOK FOR PEACE

A friend of mine once said, *"His way is easy."* While following Jesus still involves trials, suffering, and hard work, there is truth to her words. When you experience supernatural ease—when things flow in alignment—it's often a sign we are in His will. It's not always the absence of difficulty but the presence of His grace, even when things don't add up, that is a sign of His hand at work. Look for His grace to make a way, and His peace to confirm it.

> *It's not always the absence of difficulty but the presence of His grace, even when things don't add up, that is a sign of His hand at work. Look for His grace to make a way, and His peace to confirm it.*

I know how easy it is to let the noise of our daily demands drown out the peace we so desperately crave. The world will always be loud. There will always be another notification, another deadline, and another reason to rush.

But we serve a God who speaks quietly—not to hide from us, but to draw us close. He knows we can't hear Him when we are running at full speed.

So today, let's be wise enough to pause. Let's trade our frantic striving for a holy hush. You don't need to have the whole plan figured out; you simply need to be still enough to hear the One who holds the plan.

TUNING IN

Lean in.
He is speaking. And He's right there.

PRAYER:

Heavenly Father, thank You for the gift of Your guidance and the gentle ways You speak to my heart. Help me to quiet the noise around me and tune my ears to Your voice. Lord, teach me to lean into Your Spirit. Give me peace that surpasses all understanding as I step into Your purposes. I want to walk boldly, yet humbly—confident that You alone are shaping each step. May my life reflect Your love and Your glory as I use what you've entrusted to me to make a Kingdom impact. In Jesus' name, Amen.

DAY SEVEN

YOUR WORK IS NOT YOUR WORTH

SCRIPTURE:

See, I have engraved you on the palms of my hands.
—Isaiah 49:16

Have you ever had one of those days where the drive that usually fuels your work feels out of reach?

Maybe the contract fell through, the launch numbers were lower than projected, or the feedback was critical. Suddenly, your sense of worth feels dangerously tied to the visible outcome of your efforts.

Some days you wake up inspired. You're working, planning, and dreaming. You feel that rush of purpose as your work unfolds, and the results bring reward. But then there are days when the silence is loud. Doubts creep in, and you question whether your efforts are worth the cost. You start thinking, *Is this moving the needle? Is anyone noticing? Am I making a difference?*

Here's the truth every leader needs to hear: Your value doesn't fluctuate with how many people recognize your talent, buy your products, or invest in your ministry. Your worth doesn't lie in your output or the world's validation.

Your value doesn't fluctuate with how many people recognize your talent, buy your products, or invest in your ministry.

God sees you. Not just the finished product or the polished version of your work, but the unseen moments of obedience. He sees the late nights, the hard decisions made in private, and the quiet sacrifices made for the Kingdom. And He whispers: *"You are mine. You are chosen. You are secure."*

Society pressures us to use our work to seek status, convincing us that if we achieve measurable results, we will finally feel *"enough."* I know how tempting it is to chase that validation; I've tried it. I pursued prestigious roles and financial security because they felt like the smart moves at the time. But the fulfillment was fleeting.

Jesus warned us of exactly this: *"What good is it for someone to gain the whole world, yet forfeit their soul?"* (Mark 8:36).

When we use our gifts solely to impress, we might hit the goal, but we miss the purpose. We gain temporary satisfaction but lose the joy of using our gifts for His glory. It's worth pausing to take inventory: *What is your soul actually worth?*

We hustle to etch our names onto trophies, titles, and org charts—places where our standing can be erased in an instant. Deep down, we worry that if we stop achieving, we will be forgotten. But God meets that fear with His permanent promise: *"See, I have engraved you on the palms of my hands."*

Think about that for a moment. He didn't write your name in pencil or note it down somewhere to be easily erased. *Engraved.* Your name is *etched* into the hands of the God who formed the universe. *That's* how much He values you. That's the security you carry.

The same God who holds you is the One who carefully knit you together in your mother's womb (Psalm 139:13). He didn't wait for you to prove your worth at a job; He chose you before the foundations of the earth were even laid (Ephesians 1:4). He knows you so intimately that He has counted the very hairs on your head (Luke 12:7). You are not a random byproduct of the world; you are a specific, intentional design of the Creator.

Imagine waking up tomorrow and embracing who you are over what you do. Not telling others about your title or follower count, but about the One who gives your work meaning. Speak the truth He speaks over you: You are chosen. You are equipped. You are enough.

YOUR WORK IS NOT YOUR WORTH

    Instead of chasing validation, lean into the truth that your worth was never meant to be measured by your productivity. Instead of striving to be seen, rest in the fact that you are already known.
    Instead of wondering if your work matters, trust that every act of obedience is seen by the One who called you in the first place.
    Your work—your gifts, your leadership, your service—is an offering. But your identity? That is already settled.

Instead of chasing validation, lean into the truth that your worth was never meant to be measured by your productivity.

PRAYER:

Father, on the days when I feel like my efforts don't matter, help me remember that my value isn't defined by my output but by Your love and Your finished work. Give me courage to use what You've entrusted to me to bring You glory, and to find my worth in You alone. Help me to pursue You over any recognition this world could offer. Thank You for declaring me enough, just as I am. In Jesus' name, Amen.

DAY EIGHT

REFILLED

> **SCRIPTURE:**
>
> *May the God of hope fill you with all joy and peace in believing [through the experience of your faith] that by the power of the Holy Spirit you will abound in hope and overflow with confidence in His promises.* —Romans 15:13 AMP

There's a subtle narrative that dictates the pace of the modern marketplace: *busyness equals success*. If your calendar isn't color-coded chaos and your inbox isn't overflowing, are you even trying?

The endless errands, appointments, and obligations pile up like trophies—though they leave us anything but triumphant. When someone asks, *"How are you?"* it's almost instinctive to respond, *"Good... just busy,"* as if *busy* is the validation we need to prove we're doing enough...we *are* enough.

But beneath that polished answer often lies something much deeper: *exhaustion*. It's not just physical—it's emotional, mental, and spiritual.

We long to pour our gifts, leadership, and creativity into the people and projects God has entrusted to us, but the daily grind wears us down. Yet we soldier on, believing that endurance is the only option.

You tell yourself, *"One more thing, then I'll rest. Just one more push until the kids go to bed, then I'll recharge."* But the finish line keeps moving, and your reserves keep dropping. You're starting to feel like that forgotten cup of coffee left in the microwave for the third time—once warm and full of promise, now cold and overlooked.

The truth is, the weariness doesn't come all at once. It's the slow drain of demands: keeping our life sensible, the house presentable, and clean clothes accessible. Each task takes a little more out of us.

We can pour ourselves out into all the right things, but if we don't take the time to be refilled, we will eventually come up short with nothing left to give.

When we're stretched thin, our stewardship suffers. Our teams notice it. Our families feel it when we snap at our kids. We become short with colleagues, disconnected at home, and the time we're meant to spend with God—the very source of our strength—gets pushed to the margins yet again.

If this sounds familiar, take heart—you're not alone. And more importantly, you don't have to stay here.

The beauty of realizing our emptiness is that it leads us to the One who is the source of true, lasting strength. This moment of vulnerability is a place of incredible potential. The Lord doesn't scold us for running out of steam. Instead, He invites us to come to Him and let *Him* do the pouring.

Romans 15:13 reminds us that the God of hope longs to fill us—not simply to maintenance levels, but to overflowing.

Imagine starting your day not with an empty tank, but with a heart brimming with His presence. How would your day look different? What if, instead of squeezing God into your busy schedule, *you let Him reshape it entirely?*

> *The beauty of realizing our emptiness is that it leads us to the One who is the source of true, lasting strength. This moment of vulnerability is a place of incredible potential.*

God never intended for us to carry the weight of our calling alone. He knows the twists and turns of every detail in your day before you wake up. He sees the deadlines, the interruptions, and the unexpected challenges. And He offers you strength—not through sheer willpower or another cup of coffee, but through His Spirit.

When we allow God to fill us, something amazing happens. Our perspective shifts. The tasks that once felt wearisome start to feel purposeful, and work that seemed tedious turns to ease. He turns our to-do lists into acts of service, our work into worship, and our exhaustion into purpose. When we surrender our time to the One who determines our steps, even the mundane moments can be infused with His joy.

But here's the key for every steward: Your gifts can't flow effectively from a soul that's running on empty.

We need Him to fill our hearts *before* we fill our hands. We need to create space for God to do the pouring so the work we're called to do can overflow from a deep reservoir of His grace, not from a strained and exhausted spirit.

> We need Him to fill our hearts **before** we fill our hands. We need to create space for God to do the pouring so the work we're called to do can overflow from a deep reservoir of His grace, not from a strained and exhausted spirit.

So, what does that look like? It's not about adding more to your to-do list. It's about creating small pockets of stillness where God can meet you in your day.

Maybe it's quiet time with your Bible before the family wakes up. Maybe it's a prayer whispered on your way home from the office or while folding the fifth load of laundry. Whatever you choose, trust that He will meet you there. The world won't fall apart if you take time to rest in Him. Your inbox will still be there, but you'll face it with a renewed spirit and fresh perspective.

Instead of striving to get everything done, you'll find joy in simply being with God and being the leader and steward He's called you to be where it matters most.

Let go of the rush and remember, when you make time for the Lord to fill you up, you will overflow with His love and power in all that you do.

ENTRUSTED

PRAYER:

Thank You for being the God who sees me and knows exactly what I need. Help me to let go of the busyness that leaves me drained and to rest in Your presence. Fill me with Your peace, renew my joy, and remind me that my worth isn't in what I get done, but in Your love. As You fill me, let my work be an outpouring of the hope and grace You've placed in my heart. In Jesus' name, Amen.

DAY NINE

CHOOSING GOD OVER APPROVAL

> **SCRIPTURE:**
>
> Am I now trying to win the favor and approval of men, or of God? Or am I seeking to please someone? If I were still trying to be popular with men, I would not be a bond-servant of Christ.
> — Galatians 1:10 AMP

There's a weight that comes with living for the approval of others. It's an easy habit to fall into without even realizing it—choosing our words carefully so we don't offend, making decisions that keep the peace, holding back parts of ourselves to fit within the expectations of the crowd. It often disguises itself as kindness, wisdom, or even responsibility. But at its core, people-pleasing isn't about serving others well—it's about fearing rejection.

When we seek approval from people, we give them the power to determine our worth. We allow the court of public opinion to dictate our actions, often at the expense of obedience to God.

Over time, this becomes a trap—a quiet surrender of the authority given us to steward our gifts in exchange for the comfort of acceptance.

When we seek approval from people, we give them the power to determine our worth.

I've found myself there more times than I'd like to admit. Shrinking a God-gvien vision down to a more "reasonable" size to avoid criticism. Hesitating to speak truth because it might stir the waters. Second-guessing a decision I knew God had confirmed, simply because I wondered what someone else might think.

It's exhausting, isn't it? The endless pursuit of being liked, approved of, and understood.

Maybe you've felt this tension before: the pull between wanting to follow God's call and the fear of how others might perceive you.

What if they don't understand?

What if I fail publicly?

But the Gospel isn't about fitting in. It's about standing firm. Kingdom stewardship is about choosing *obedience* over popularity, *faithfulness* over comfort, and *purpose* over applause.

When we live to please people, we end up enslaved to their opinions. When we live to please God, we step into *freedom*.

The world will always have an opinion about what you *should* do, how you *should* live, and what is "wise" or "acceptable." But the world doesn't hold your calling—God does. He has entrusted you with specific gifts, passions, and convictions, not to be silenced by fear but to be deployed in faith.

Kingdom stewardship is about choosing **obedience** *over popularity,* **faithfulness** *over comfort, and* **purpose** *over applause.*

If you find yourself hesitating today, caught in the tension between obedience to God and acceptance from others, let this be your reminder: Their approval was never the goal. God's voice is the only one that truly matters, and the assignment He has placed on your life does not need a committee's agreement to move forward. It only needs your obedience.

So, step forward. Not timidly, not apologetically, but with the confidence of a steward who answers to one Master. Release the weight of people-pleasing and walk in the freedom that comes from knowing you already have the only approval that matters.

CHOOSING GOD OVER APPROVAL

PRAYER:

Lord, free me from the trap of seeking approval from others. Give me the boldness to follow You wholeheartedly, without hesitation or fear of man. Let my life be marked by obedience to Your call, not the expectations of those around me. Remind me that Your approval is enough, and help me to walk in the freedom and confidence of knowing I am fully loved, fully seen, and fully called by You. In Jesus' name, Amen.

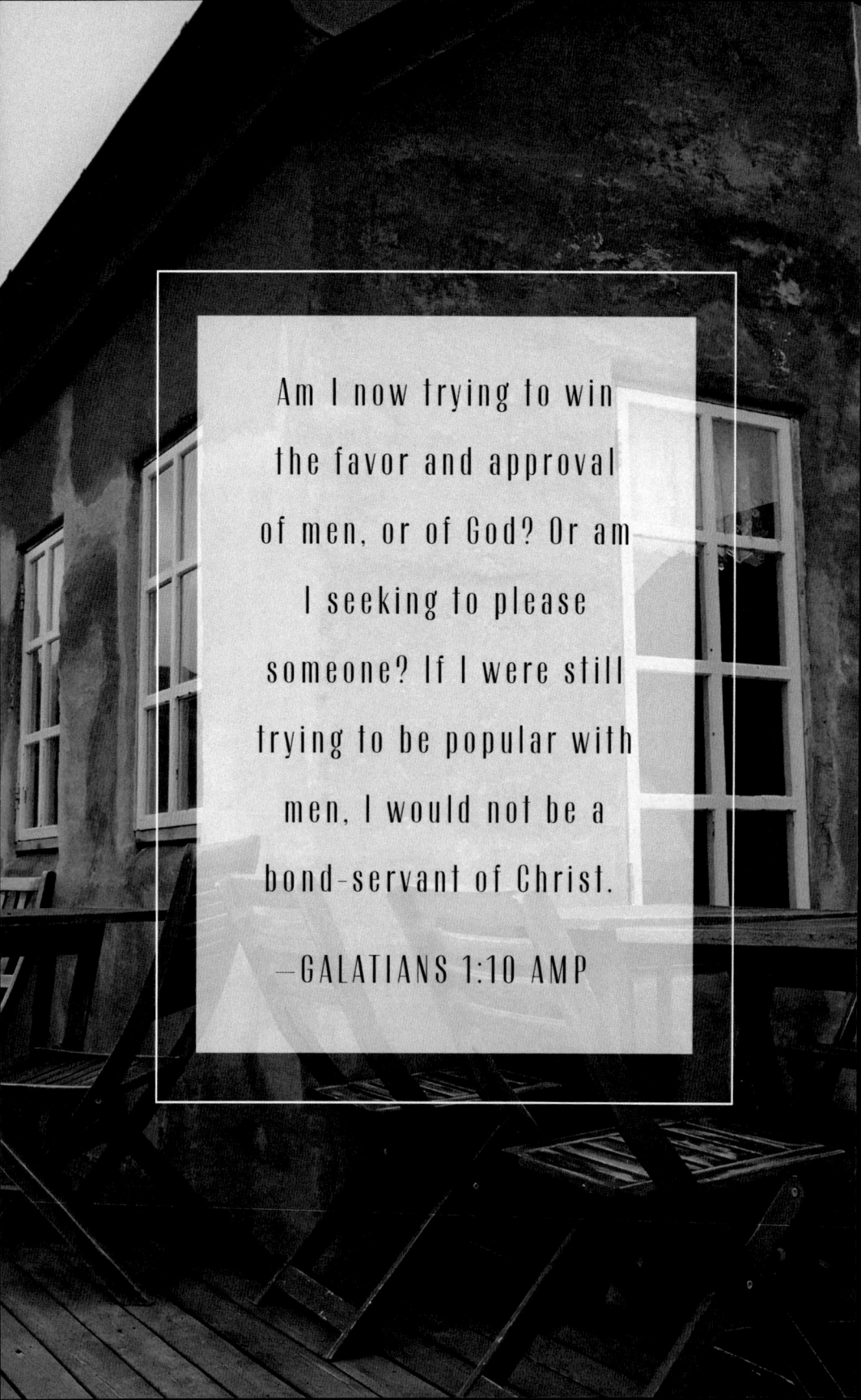

> Am I now trying to win the favor and approval of men, or of God? Or am I seeking to please someone? If I were still trying to be popular with men, I would not be a bond-servant of Christ.
>
> —GALATIANS 1:10 AMP

DAY TEN

CALLED TO HIS PURPOSE, NOT OUR PLATFORM

SCRIPTURE:

But seek first his kingdom and his righteousness, and all these things will be given to you as well. —Matthew 6:33

In a world that celebrates the hustle of empire-building and self-made success, it's easy to slip into rhythms of self-driven ambition. But how often do we pause to ask ourselves, *"Is this path truly in alignment with God's will, or is it just my agenda dressed up as 'God's plan'?"*

The desire to make an impact and leave a mark isn't wrong. God places dreams and ambitions within us for a reason. But not every good idea is a *God idea*. Not every strategy is a Kingdom assignment.

So how do we know the difference?

Human ambition usually asks, *'What can I build, own, or control?'* God's plan asks, *'Who can I serve?'* The shift is subtle but significant: moving from impact for the sake of ego, to impact for the sake of the Kingdom.

For me, ideas can pour out faster than anyone can keep up with. I'll map out plans that seem perfect—dreams I'm sure will come to fruition and provide more for my family. But I've spent *years* learning that just because a plan looks successful on paper doesn't mean it's God's assignment for me. I could chart every step, envision every milestone, and still miss the quiet invitation to surrender my agenda for His anointing.

The thing is: anyone can launch a business or lead an organization. But true ministry—the kind that shifts atmospheres and changes lives—only happens when led by the Holy Spirit.

So if I catch myself gripping too tightly to my own formula for success, that's my clue. It's the moment I pause and ask, *"Am I making space for God's voice, or just asking Him to bless my plans, and assuming His Kingdom will follow?"*

Scripture calls us to *"seek first His Kingdom."* Jesus reminds us that when we prioritize God's agenda and righteousness, He takes care of our needs. This truth applies not only to our daily provisions but also to our ambitions—when we seek Him first, He aligns our desires with His greater purpose.

Am I making space for God's voice, or just asking Him to bless my plans, and assuming His Kingdom will follow?

So, when was the last time you paused to ask, *"Lord, what do You want me to do for You?"*—and truly meant it?

Asking that question is essential because unchecked ambition loves to justify compromise. We start thinking, *if I just bend a little here, I can do more for God later.* Yet God never calls us to sacrifice integrity for influence. His purpose is always marked by obedience and trust, not shortcuts.

THREE WAYS TO ALIGN WITH HIS PATH:

Here are three practical ways to align your ambition with His assignment:

1. CHECK YOUR MOTIVES

Ask yourself, *"Is this about advancing my name or His Kingdom?"*

God's calling is service-focused, while personal ambition is often self-centered. Are you willing to be a *"nobody"* in the body of Christ? Are you willing to lead without the spotlight, secure in the knowledge that you don't need titles or positions to prove your worth as one already chosen by your Creator? When we hold our positions loosely and serve without seeking attention, we free ourselves from comparison and pride, resting in Christ rather than the fleeting approval of others.

When our motives are surrendered, ambition aligns with purpose and can become powerful.

Are you willing to be a "nobody" in the body of Christ? Are you willing to lead without the spotlight, secure in the knowledge that you don't need titles or positions to prove your worth as one already chosen by your Creator?

2. TRUST HIS TIMING

When we feel the temptation to self-promote to ensure our work is seen, we must remember: If God has called us, He will open doors—ones we don't have to scramble to keep open. This assurance allows us to run confidently in His direction, knowing we won't need to strive excessively beyond His leading, manipulate, or compromise to force an outcome.

Trusting His timing doesn't mean we sit back passively waiting for success to fall into our laps. It means we faithfully steward what He has given us today while trusting Him to establish our steps for tomorrow.

God doesn't need us to build a platform for ourselves; He knows the exact moment to lift us up. When we finally surrender our gifts for His glory rather than our gain, our focus shifts from self to God. This leaves us free to serve others with more joy and purpose along the way.

3. EVALUATE DEPENDENCE

Are you trying to sustain what *you've* started, or allowing God to sustain what *He's* begun?

There's a peace that comes from knowing we don't have to "make it happen" in our own strength. When He's the CEO, we rest in Him. We trust Him to provide the resources, the network, and the opportunities needed to fulfill the plan.

We don't have to stifle our ambition; we need to sanctify it. God gave you that drive, that fire, and that ability to dream big. But He didn't give it to you so you could burn out trying to build a name for yourself. He gave it to you because, when directed by the Holy Spirit, it becomes powerful fuel that burns for God's Kingdom.

The Lord reminds me daily that it is possible to be both ambitious and anointed—as long as our ambitions are surrendered to Him.

So today, let's stop striving to be seen and start striving to be obedient. Ask yourself: *"Am I truly pursuing God's purpose? Am I willing to let go of my plans for His?"* When we allow our drive to align with His will, we step out of the exhaustion of self-promotion and into the peace of Kingdom impact. And that is a life worth pursuing.

CALLED TO HIS PURPOSE, NOT OUR PLATFORM

PRAYER:

Father God, align my heart with Yours. Reveal any ill ambition within me that does not serve Your Kingdom and replace it with a hunger for advancing Your Kingdom alone. Lead me to release my plans and trust fully in Yours, knowing that You have called me to make Your name known, not my own. Strengthen my faith to let go of my need for recognition, so I can serve with integrity and humility. Help me run the race You have set before me, keeping my eyes on Jesus and the work You've anointed me to do. I choose Your peace over my performance. In Jesus' name, Amen.

> But seek first his kingdom and his righteousness, and all these things will be given to you as well.
>
> —MATTHEW 6:33

DAY ELEVEN

COURAGE OVER CONFIDENCE

> **SCRIPTURE:**
>
> *David also said to Solomon his son, "Be strong and courageous, and do the work. Do not be afraid or discouraged, for the Lord God, my God, is with you. He will not fail you or forsake you until all the work for the service of the temple of the Lord is finished."*
> —1 Chronicles 28:20

I used to think I needed confidence before stepping into what God was calling me to do. Confidence felt like the secret weapon of high achievers—the ones who walk into a crowded room without hesitation, the entrepreneurs who pitch with unwavering certainty.

I've since learned that confidence *isn't* what moves us forward. Courage is. We often confuse the two, but they are not the same.

Confidence is a feeling. It's a belief based on track record and experience. It's the internal assurance that usually only comes *after* we've faced the unknown and come out on the other side.

Courage, on the other hand, is what gets us started in the first place. It's the choice to act before we know how something will turn out, before we have the data. It's stepping out even when our knees are shaking. Courage is a prerequisite for action. We don't wait around for it; we step into it, even when confidence has yet to catch up.

Think back to grade school when the teacher asked a question, and you hesitated before raising your hand. It wasn't the sheer act of lifting your arm that was daunting—it was the uncertainty of what might happen next. *What if I get the answer wrong? What if everyone looks at me?* Acting despite that uncertainty—that's courage. The confidence comes later, once you realize you survived the risk and learned from the result.

Isn't it just like us to get this backwards? We tell ourselves we need assurance first—proof that the business will scale or the ministry will grow—before we muster the courage to move. We allow our feelings to dictate our strategy, convincing ourselves that obedience can wait until we feel "ready."

But nowhere in Scripture are we told to feel confident, *then* act. God asks us to put our confidence in Him, then act. If we're always waiting for clarity, we might miss the calling.

When King David commissioned his son Solomon to build the temple, he didn't tell him to wait until he felt like an expert builder. He *didn't* say, *"Get all your questions answered, make sure you have a five-step plan, and then move forward."* No, David told him: *"Be strong and courageous, and do the work"* (1 Chronicles 28:20a).

Solomon had never built a temple before, and he didn't have years of experience to draw on. He had to step forward in faith, trusting that God would equip him along the way.

Maybe that's where you are today. You feel a stirring to step into something new—to create, to lead, to start, to speak. But instead of moving forward, you're waiting—waiting for a guarantee that it will all work out.

Can I gently remind you? Assurance isn't the goal. Confidence isn't the goal. *Obedience is.* And obedience often requires us to step out before we see the full picture.

Assurance isn't the goal.
Confidence isn't the goal. Obedience is.

Courage is saying "yes" even when you don't have all the answers. It's doing the hard thing, even when fear lists all the reasons you shouldn't. But when you push through that fear, something shifts. Every act of courage plants the seeds of confidence for the future. God knows our fears, and He doesn't waste them. He uses them to shape our faith, drawing us closer to Him in the process. Because faith isn't built in the comfort zone; it's forged in the risk of surrender.

If you want to grow, to step into the life He's calling you to, there comes a moment when staying where you are feels more painful than stepping into the unknown. Sometimes, the ache of settling for safe but unfulfilled can be far greater than any risk we could take.

Sometimes, the ache of settling for safe but unfulfilled can be far greater than any risk we could take.

So, what's the assignment God has placed before you? Is it joining the worship team? Writing the book? Starting the business? Speaking up when it matters?

It's time to stop waiting for confidence to arrive. Feelings are fickle, and waiting until you *feel ready* is a strategy for stagnation.

Remember the maxim: courage isn't the absence of fear, it's the choice to move forward despite it.

God isn't asking you to *feel* capable. He's asking you to trust that *He is capable*. Your past experience, your education, your resume—none of those define what's possible when God is leading. You don't have to know exactly how it will turn out. You simply need to take the next step.

The enemy would love nothing more than for you to stay stuck in the cycle of inaction—waiting, hesitating, questioning if you're really ready. Because as long as you delay, you won't step into the fullness of what God has for you. But God's plans don't come with a *"maybe later"* or *"one day"* stamped on them. They're for right now.

Waiting until you feel ready is a strategy for stagnation.

ENTRUSTED

So let's choose courage today. Let's take the next step, even if it feels small. And remember, what God has placed inside of you—that longing, that holy nudge—may be only one step of courage away from bearing fruit. The world is desperate for believers who will step out in faith, fully leaning on the strength of their Father and the certainty of His unchanging promises.

Remember, what God has placed inside of you—that longing, that holy nudge—may be only one step of courage away from bearing fruit.

PRAYER:

Thank You for being with me in every courageous step. When fear tries to hold me back, remind me that feelings are fickle, but Your promises never fail. Give me the courage to move forward, trusting that the fruit of doing hard things is worth it. Help me to lean on Your strength, not my own, and to walk boldly in faith, knowing You are with me. In Jesus' name, Amen.

DAY TWELVE

THE POWER OF YOUR WORDS

SCRIPTURE:

Death and life are in the power of the tongue...
—Proverbs 18:21 AMP

We've all heard the childhood phrase, *"Sticks and stones may break my bones, but words will never hurt me."* It's a defense mechanism we've taught children to help them shake off hurtful comments. But as adults, we know the truth: words carry weight. A single piece of feedback can crush morale, and a well-timed encouragement can ignite a team's performance.

I once heard about an experiment that reshaped my understanding of this principle. In a school, two identical plants were placed in the same environment with equal access to sunlight and water. Students were told to repeat only the kind words they had received or thought to themselves to one plant. To the other, they could repeat only harsh or discouraging words they had received or thought to themselves.

The results were striking. The plant that received affirmation grew healthy, taller, and even leaned away from the other plant. Meanwhile, the plant exposed to harsh words struggled, appearing less vibrant and slightly shriveled. This simple experiment is a vivid reminder: words influence the environment in which we—and our work—either flourish or wither.

Our words truly hold power, and that truth should stop us in our tracks. Every word we speak carries weight. And while our words do not hold the sovereign power of God's, as image-bearers, we reflect our Creator's authority and hold influence over ourselves and others. Words aren't just fleeting sounds; they have the power to build momentum for the Kingdom, shape culture, or tear down what we're trying to build.

This is especially true in our stewardship. It's not just the words of others that impact us—it's the words we speak to ourselves. Too often, we fail to recognize the power of our own voice in shaping our reality. But one of the most important meetings you have every day is the one that happens inside your own head.

When we speak about our work, our calling, and our abilities, we are either affirming or denying the gifts God has entrusted to us.

Are you declaring that you are equipped, worthy, and that your work brings value? Or are you letting self-doubt cloud your narrative?

What if we believed that every word had the potential to shape a life, encourage a weary heart, or water a long-dormant dream? Psalm 19:14 NIV says: *"May these words of my mouth and this meditation of my heart be pleasing in your sight, Lord, my Rock and my Redeemer."*

How comforting—and convicting—it is to consider that every word we speak is heard by a God who listens. Not one word is lost in the wind; not one is unaccounted for.

As a leader and a steward, the words you speak over yourself and your God-given gifts are like seeds planted in the soil of your mind. With every declaration—whether of faith or of doubt—you are nurturing something. Your words will eventually take root, shaping your perceptions and actions.

With every declaration—whether of faith or of doubt—you are nurturing something. Your words will eventually take root, shaping your perceptions and actions.

Consider what areas of your life need rejuvenation. Are there ideas or gifts you've hidden away, uncertain of their potential or worth? Start speaking life into them, knowing that your voice sets the stage for what happens next.

When we look back to Genesis, after God spoke the very world into existence, the enemy approached Eve with a question that has since echoed through history: *"Did God actually say..."* (Genesis 3:1)? Notice, he didn't outright deny God's power; he simply cast doubt on God's spoken Word.

He does the same today. He plants seeds of uncertainty, making us question whether we are truly capable or if we are who God says we are. And when we speak self-limiting words over ourselves, we inadvertently echo that same question, partnering with the enemy's doubt of the goodness and sufficiency of God's Word over us.

Proverbs 23:7 (AMP) reminds us: *"For as he thinks in his heart, so is he [in behavior—one who manipulates]."*

If you're struggling with feelings of inadequacy or frustration in your work, take a moment to evaluate your internal narrative. Are you believing lies about your capacity?

We cannot let those lies roam free. Instead, we are called to *'take every thought captive to obey Christ'* (2 Corinthians 10:5). We must intercept these doubts at the source—in our minds—refusing to let a fleeting fear become a spoken reality.

So let's shift our thinking. Instead of saying, *"I'll never be good enough,"* declare, *"God has equipped me for this purpose."* Rather than feeling defeated by, *"I'll never succeed,"* speak forth, *"God will provide for the vision He gave me."*

Our words reveal the state of our faith. If our language is filled with negativity, it sabotages our execution and shows there may be fears or wounds God wants to heal. Knowing what we focus on grows; let's be intentional about our language, reflecting on the truth God speaks over us.

Let's be leaders who speak life–not just over our teams or families, but over our own calling. Because what we whisper in the quiet places shapes the way we lead in public.

Speak boldly. Speak victory. And watch as God brings forth fruit from the gifts He has placed in your hands.

ENTRUSTED

PRAYER:

Father, thank You for the gift of words. Help me to be mindful of the power my words carry. May Your Holy Spirit guide my thoughts and my tongue, leading me to speak life, truth, and peace over myself and over my work and the assignment You've entrusted to me. Teach me to declare Your promises rather than my fears. Use my voice to build Your Kingdom and to steward the influence You've entrusted to me. In Jesus' name, Amen.

DAY THIRTEEN

TRUSTING BEYOND OUR COMFORT ZONE

> **SCRIPTURE:**
>
> Then Moses said to the Lord, "Please, Lord, I am not a man of words (eloquent, fluent), neither before nor since You have spoken to Your servant; for I am slow of speech and tongue." The Lord said to him, "Who has made man's mouth? Or who makes the mute or the deaf, or the seeing or the blind? Is it not I, the Lord? Now then go, and I, even I, will be with your mouth, and will teach you what you shall say." But he said, "Please my Lord, send the message [of rescue to Israel] by [someone else,] whomever else You will [choose]. —Exodus 4:10-13 AMP

Have you ever sensed a directive from God to step forward, but your immediate internal reaction was, *"Anything but that, Lord"?* You want to follow Him and allow Him to use you, yet the specific assignment He is handing you feels completely out of your wheelhouse. You're all too aware of your limitations. Your doubts looming like roadblocks. And you can't help but wonder, *Does He really want to use someone like me?*

Moses knew exactly how that felt. Here he was, a man who had nearly seen the God of the universe face to face, being called to lead the Israelites out of Egypt. But all he could see was his own liability—his stuttering, his inadequacy, his *not-enoughness*. And his response echoes the hesitation many of us feel: *I'm not equipped for this, Lord! Please, send someone more qualified.*

It's so easy to focus on our weaknesses, isn't it?

In the midst of His calling, our default reaction is to conduct a personal risk assessment. We stack up all the reasons why we aren't the right person for the job. We try to shrink back, hoping God will delegate the responsibility to someone else.

But God doesn't relent, and He doesn't wait for our skills to match the assignment. Instead, He assures us that He'll equip us every step of the way.

Think of Moses, trembling at the thought of speaking before Pharaoh—a massive leadership assignment requiring high-stakes negotiation, I'm sure. A man who stumbled over his words was filled with insecurities and certainly questioning why on earth God would choose *him*. This is the same man who'd seen God's miracles firsthand, yet he couldn't shake the belief that he wasn't up for the task.

We do that, too, don't we? God has shown Himself faithful in our lives time and time again, yet we still find ourselves doubting.

God wasn't demanding that Moses suddenly become a world-class orator. The success of the mission wasn't dependent on Moses's natural ability; it was dependent on God's divine power moving through human frailty.

It's the same for us.

Throughout Scripture, God chooses those who feel unqualified—not because of their skills, but because His power is revealed in human weakness (2 Corinthians 12:9; 1 Corinthians 1:27).

Please hear this. When we say *yes* to God, we give up the right to put conditions on how He uses us.

When we say yes to God, we give up the right to put conditions on how He uses us.

The most fulfilling work comes when we align our willingness with *His* plans, even when it demands we step out of our expertise and into dependency on Him. This requires surrendering our preferences for safety and trusting His wisdom over our own. It means letting go of control and letting Him work in ways that may take us far beyond our comfort zones.

While feelings of inadequacy can weigh on us, each assignment He gives is grounded in *His* power at work. We are mere vessels.

I relate to Moses deeply. Public speaking, my biggest fear, looms large over me. As an introvert, I find comfort in being unseen. And yet, saying *yes* to God has often meant embracing moments of high visibility and discomfort, aligning my obedience with His purposes, and leaning into roles that challenge everything I believe about my own ability.

The most fulfilling work comes when we align our willingness with His plans, even when it demands we step out of our expertise and into dependency on Him. This requires surrendering our preferences for safety and trusting His wisdom over our own.

Just as the Lord empowered Moses to lead a nation, He will empower you. He will equip you for the tasks He ordains, even if they feel beyond your current pay grade.

Even in Moses' doubts and resistance, God never abandoned him, and that same promise is yours. You can trust His refining work and know His grace will always meet you precisely in those moments of fear and be enough.

When fear tries to hold you back, remember that God's grace is sufficient to overcome your limitations. It's precisely in this discomfort that we experience the fullness of His transformative work and find His strength sufficient.

Don't wait until you feel qualified. Step out, and watch God make up the difference.

ENTRUSTED

PRAYER:

Dear Lord, in my moments of hesitation and fear, remind me of Your unwavering presence. Grant me the courage to say yes to Your calling, trusting that You equip me even when I feel inadequate. May Your strength shine through my weakness, and may I find peace in Your guiding hand. In Jesus' name, Amen.

DAY FOURTEEN

FROM HUSTLE TO HOLY REST

14

SCRIPTURE:

There remains, then, a Sabbath-rest for the people of God; for anyone who enters God's rest also rests from their works, just as God did from his. —Hebrews 4:9-10

It's 9:00 PM. The notifications are still pinging. The to-do list you made this morning is now longer than when you started, and your mind is already racing with plans for the day ahead.

Sound familiar? We've been conditioned to believe that slowing down means we're losing ground—that we're slacking. In a culture that glorifies the "grind," we convince ourselves that if we stop, we'll get passed by. But this mindset is exhausting, unsustainable, and not the life God calls us to live.

What if the breakthrough you're longing for isn't at the finish line of your striving, but in the quiet surrender of rest? What if what we've been trying to steward is the very thing we need to release?

What if the breakthrough you're longing for isn't at the finish line of your striving, but in the quiet surrender of rest? What if what we've been trying to steward is the very thing we need to release?

From the beginning, God designed rest as part of the order of creation. He worked for six days, then rested on the seventh to establish a pattern for us to follow. In today's 24/7 economy, the idea of Sabbath rest can feel outdated, even impossible. Who has time to step away when there's so much to do?

But the principle of Sabbath rest is an offer far greater than the temporary relief of a day off. Though often dismissed as irrelevant, it is a timeless gift of wisdom. It's a declaration of trust. A beautiful invitation to peace. An open door to lay down your striving and trust God enough to pause, even when there's work left undone, and acknowledge that He is the One who holds it all together.

The Sabbath wasn't given to restrict your productivity; it was given to protect your soul.

As a tangible reminder of His provision in the Old Testament, God provided daily manna when the Israelites were in the wilderness. He instructed them to gather enough for six days but to rest on the seventh, promising that He would supply exactly what they needed. Yet some, driven by fear and self-reliance, tried to gather more—believing that securing provision depended on their hustle rather than on God's faithfulness. In doing so, they revealed their struggle to trust the Provider.

How often do we do the same?

We tell ourselves, *Just one more thing*. Pushing beyond what God intended, we view rest as a luxury we have to earn. We rationalize our overextension, telling ourselves that peace is waiting right behind the next milestone. Yet somehow, the finish line keeps moving, and true rest remains elusive.

This isn't a mere scheduling problem; it's a spiritual tactic to keep us enslaved. The enemy wants to keep you bound to the treadmill of performance, seeking fulfillment in what you accomplish rather than who you are in Christ.

If you place the weight of your peace on your performance, hear this: We cannot live as slaves to our gifts and not expect them to become burdens.

When we ignore the divine rhythm of rest, our leadership becomes less effective, our creativity dries up, and our stewardship suffers.

We cannot live as slaves to our gifts and not expect them to become burdens.

Isaiah 26:3 (AMP) says: *"You will keep in perfect and constant peace the one whose mind is steadfast [that is, committed and focused on You—in both inclination and character], because he trusts and takes refuge in You [with hope and confident expectation]."*

This rest is available to every believer—a refusal to carry the weight of the world because we trust the One who holds it. Peace sustained doesn't come from checking off every box or finally feeling in control. It comes from a perspective shift: surrendering control to the true Provider of our lives.

This kind of trust guards our hearts and minds, even when deadlines loom, and tasks feel endless. It is more than a physical break—it is a soul-deep rest that grounds us back in Him when we loosen our grip. And when we fix our eyes on Him, we find the steady assurance we have been craving, no matter what swirls around us."

PRACTICAL STEPS TOWARD SOUL-DEEP REST

If your heart feels weary and worn, here are a few intentional steps to lean in to God's invitation to rest:

1. ESTABLISH STRATEGIC PAUSES

Designate intentional time in your day (even if it's only 10 minutes) to disconnect from the chaos and lean into God's presence. Recalibrate your soul through worship, prayer, and Scripture. Let those moments be your refuge of renewal.

2. RELEASE THE WEIGHT OF OUTCOMES

Remember, rest doesn't make you lazy or irresponsible. It's a courageous act of surrender, trusting that God is working on your behalf even when you aren't active.

3. ANCHOR YOUR IDENTITY IN HIM

Speak His truth over your heart daily. Your value isn't found in your output, your net worth, or your title. It is found in the unshakable reality of being God's child.

There is a better way to work—one that doesn't require you to burn out to break through. So, imagine what your life and leadership would look like if you stepped off the treadmill and worked from a place of abundance rather than exhaustion.

Your gifts would become an offering that flows freely and powerfully. You would still work hard, but not out of a need to prove yourself or chase the next finish line. Your creativity would flourish from renewal, not desperation. And your everyday peace wouldn't depend on your circumstances but on the steadfast love of your Creator.

Imagine what your life and leadership would look like if you stepped off the treadmill and worked from a place of abundance rather than exhaustion.

When you surrender your gifts, your time, and your ambition to God, He transforms those same worn-out gifts into blessings that flow from His grace—not your striving. The weight lifts, and what remains is a life marked by His peace.

FROM HUSTLE TO HOLY REST

PRAYER:

Heavenly Father, thank You for the gift of rest. Help me to release the burdens I was never meant to carry and to trust in Your provision. Teach me to pause in my busy day and to find my worth in You, not in my work or achievements. Renew my heart and mind so that I can live from a place of peace, creating and working for Your glory. In Jesus' name, Amen

You will keep in perfect and constant peace the one whose mind is steadfast [that is, committed and focused on You—in both inclination and character], because he trusts and takes refuge in You [with hope and confident expectation].

—MATTHEW 6:33 AMP

DAY FIFTEEN

NAYSAYERS

15

> **SCRIPTURE:**
>
> *I am carrying on a great project and cannot go down. Why should the work stop while I leave it and go down to you?*
> *—Nehemiah 6:3*

Have you ever noticed that the moment you commit to something new, a wave of doubt and negativity crashes over you? For leaders, entrepreneurs, and creatives, this experience is all too familiar. We ignite with passion for the assignment God has placed in our hearts, only to suddenly find ourselves surrounded by voices questioning our abilities and the practicality of the plan.

Perhaps you're trying to launch a new business, pivot your career, or start a ministry. If you're stepping into the unknown, chances are you've faced opposition.

Well-meaning peers might praise your ideas while strongly urging you to "be realistic" or stick to the safe path. Those tiny jabs of doubt can sting, even when, deep down, you *know* that this calling is from God.

To combat this, I often remind myself: Opposition confirms opportunity. Resistance gives us a choice—to fortify our faith or crumble under pressure.

Consider Nehemiah. He was tasked with rebuilding the walls of Jerusalem amidst relentless opposition. He faced ridicule, threats, and political maneuvering, but he didn't cower.

Instead of engaging with the naysayers, he refused to give their empty words any airtime. He directed his energy into leading and motivating his team, keeping his focus on the assignment and the purpose behind his work. Nehemiah understood that his time was a resource belonging to God, and he refused to squander it on voices that didn't share the vision.

Critics often project their own insecurities onto us. They likely haven't stepped out of their own comfort zones, which blinds them to the fruitful possibilities you see. The negativity we encounter rarely comes from those who understand our journey; it comes from the spectators—strangers and family alike. But remember: someone else's doubt holds no power unless you give it permission.

Instead of allowing their limited perspective to dictate your path, trust in God's guidance and the gifts He has placed within you. Like Nehemiah, direct your energy back toward the assignment entrusted to you. Surround yourself with supportive, faith-filled allies who share your vision, faith, and understand the cost of the journey.

Someone else's doubt holds no power unless you give it permission.

It's natural to view this pushback as a barrier to your calling.

But what if the very thing trying to stop you is actually what strengthens you?

Consider the way nature handles resistance. A tree, when faced with wind and storms, drives its roots deeper, grounding itself to reach new heights. A river stone, under the relentless force of rushing water, is shaped and polished. An airplane rises against the wind, not with it, using that resistance to defy gravity and reach incredible altitudes.

We, too, are designed to rise through opposition. Challenges don't just threaten our progress—they catalyze our growth. They force us to deepen our roots in Christ, refining our character in ways comfort never could. If we allow it, opposition shifts our perspective and ultimately leads us on a more fulfilling journey.

The world may see your aspirations as foolish, but God has a higher view. He sees the Kingdom impact that will come from your faithfulness.

So, embrace the challenge. Let the doubts of others become stepping stones rather than stumbling blocks. Allow this season to shape your journey into one of resilience, purpose, and unwavering

NAYSAYERS

faith as you walk boldly in the calling God has placed on your life.

You are chosen and uniquely gifted to make an impact. Stay on the wall. Do the work. Steward well what has been entrusted to you.

PRAYER:

Lord, thank You for the dreams and visions You've placed within me. Help me discern the voice of doubt from Your guiding hand. When criticism or negativity surrounds me, grant me the strength to rise above it and the focus of Nehemiah. Remind me of who I am in Christ—chosen, capable, and called. Empower me to persevere through challenges, trusting in Your perfect provision and Your defense. May I lean into Your calling and emerge stronger, glorifying You in every step of the journey. In Jesus' name, Amen.

Challenges don't just threaten our progress—they catalyze our growth. They force us to deepen our roots in Christ, refining our character in ways comfort never could.

DAY SIXTEEN

CO-CREATOR

16

> **SCRIPTURE:**
>
> *Let us make human beings in our image, make them reflecting our nature...* —Genesis 1:26 MSG

We all have an innate desire to create. Perhaps you're a photographer capturing the world through your lens, a graphic designer weaving visuals into stories, or an architect envisioning a new skyline.

Each of us holds a unique gift—a pull within us desiring to create in such a way that connects us to our Creator.

In the grand narrative of creation, every star, every mountain, and every living creature stands as a testament to our God, the ultimate Architect. The universe itself is God's portfolio—filled with artistry, precision, and imagination.

Yet among all His creations, *we* are the crowning glory, gifted with the extraordinary ability to create in His image.

Isn't that remarkable?

We are not mere spectators in this world; we are active participants, called to echo the creativity and innovation of the One who formed us.

However, in our results-driven world, creativity often gets tangled in the web of productivity and profit. It feels like our gifts are only valued if they bring in immediate monetary gain or societal approval. We reduce innovation to a transaction—a means to an end.

Yet as children of God and stewards, our capacity to build and create is far more than a tool for economic success. It is a sacred conduit that leads us back to the heart of our Creator. When we embrace our gifts as acts of devotion, we tap into a deeper joy and purpose that transcends the limitations of worldly expectations.

As children of God, and stewards, our capacity to build and create is far more than a tool for economic success. It is a sacred conduit that leads us back to the heart of our Creator.

Think back to your childhood when imagination flowed freely, and creativity felt effortless. Do you remember the joy of losing yourself in play? Where boundaries faded, and possibilities were endless? You had the power to be, do, and create anything your little heart desired. God rejoices in that kind of *unrestrained creativity*, and He invites us to reclaim that childlike wonder.

But as we navigate adulthood, the pressures of scalability and profit often stifle our natural creative instincts. We find ourselves caught in a cycle of comparison and risk management, doubting the worth of any endeavor that doesn't promise an immediate return.

Take a moment to reflect on what ignites your passion. Is it the thrill of solving a problem? The joy of sharing your art with others? The desire to express your unique perspective through the spoken word? Or the simple satisfaction of building something excellent with your own hands?

When we peel back the layers of expectation, we discover that our creativity is a divine gift—an expression of our identity as image-bearers.

Our creativity is a divine gift—an expression of our identity as image-bearers.

As we engage in our work, we are setting out on a journey that mirrors the divine act of creation. Just as God ordered the chaos and crafted the world with purpose and intention, so too can we approach our endeavors with a sense of divine alignment.

CO-CREATOR

Whether we find ourselves in the boardroom, the shop, or the studio, our work becomes a form of communion with God. We use our hands to shape, our minds to strategize, and our voices to lead—each act serving as an offering back to our Creator.

Let's choose to view our gifts as sacred offerings—not as mere tasks to be justified by the bottom line.

When we release the weight of outcomes and simply create, we are left with an invitation back to the heart of our Creator—the One who designed us to create for connection, purpose, and joy.

In God's presence, our creativity begins to flourish. This is where we uncover a wellspring of fulfillment that goes beyond the accolades of the world. This is where true joy lies—in the act of co-laboring with our Creator, allowing Him to work through us as we revel in the process rather than fixating on the outcome.

So, as you navigate your creative journey, remember this: You are a beloved child of the first Entrepreneur. You carry His likeness within you, and your gifts are meant to reflect His glory. Embrace your creativity as an act of worship. Allow your designs, your strategies, and your leadership to draw you closer to His heart.

PRAYER:

Heavenly Father, thank You for the gift of creativity—a reflection of Your divine nature. Help me align my ambitions to Your will and embrace my creative passions as acts of worship. May my gifts lead me into a deeper connection with You, allowing me to find true fulfillment in the process of co-creating with You as I invite You into my work. In Jesus' name, Amen.

Let us make human beings in our image, make them reflecting our nature...

—GENESIS 1:26 MSG

DAY SEVENTEEN

MARKETPLACE MINISTRY

SCRIPTURE:

...But as for me and my household, we will serve the Lord.
—Joshua 24:15

Do you ever stop and ask yourself if what you're doing truly makes a difference in God's Kingdom? Maybe you've looked at pastors or missionaries in far-off places, pouring their lives into ministry, and thought, *Does what I do even compare?*

For so long, I believed there were two categories of work: sacred and secular. Church work? Sacred. Everything else? Just a means to pay the bills.

I figured if I really loved God, I needed to be in full-time ministry because surely that's where the real impact happened. So I went to Bible college, thinking it would bring clarity. But instead of finding direction, I felt stuck—lost in the in-between. I kept waiting for my *"official"* ministry assignment to validate my calling, but it never came. And with every year that passed, the nagging feeling remained: *Am I missing it?*

Maybe you've felt that way too—as if what you're doing isn't enough because it doesn't have a spiritual title attached to it.

But God never meant for us to separate work and worship. He wove purpose into both. The very first thing God did after creating Adam was give him a job—tending the Garden. Before sin ever entered the world, there was work. It was never meant to be a curse; it was designed to be an extension of worship.

You don't have to be a pastor or missionary to do meaningful work. And let's be honest, having a church job doesn't automatically make someone holier.

There is no hierarchy to holiness.

Holiness isn't defined by a job description. God is as present in boardrooms as He is in prayer rooms. He is as intentional in hospitals, on construction sites, and in your home as He is in pulpits.

It's not *where* you work—it's *how* you work and *who* you're working for. Ministry doesn't have to be your job title, but your job title—whatever it is—*is your ministry*. It's all sacred ground when you invite Him into it.

This truth comes alive in a declaration many of us know well: *"As for me and my house, we will serve the Lord"* (Joshua 24:15).

HEBREW:

From the root abad, *avodah* means work, service, or worship. It encompasses labor, ministry, or acts of devotion, whether sacred or secular—expressing both practical service and whole-hearted dedication to God's purposes.[2]

When Joshua speaks of *"serving,"* he uses the Hebrew word *Avodah*—a rich, multi-dimensional word that means *work, worship, and service all at once.* No separation, no compartments. The same word that describes tending the fields also describes worshiping God in the temple.

Isn't that awesome?

It offers us an integrated faith, where your Monday grind and your Sunday praise flow from the same foundation.

When we embrace this mindset, everything shifts. The marketplace becomes more than simply a place to make a profit or earn a paycheck. It becomes *a gateway into our culture*—a culture desperate for truth, hope, and integrity.

Some people may never walk into a church, but they can still encounter God through the way you work with care, excellence, and intention.

MARKETPLACE MINISTRY

What if your gifts are God's way of planting seeds in places only you can reach? What if your integrity through a simple encounter speaks louder than a sermon?

Your work isn't just a means to an end; it's a living act of *avodah*. So, whether you're leading a team, managing your household, or painting a canvas, you have the opportunity to reflect His character.

You may not always see the immediate fruit of your efforts, but trust that God is working through you to bring hope and transformation to those you encounter.

PRAYER:

Lord, thank You for the unique gifts You've placed in me and for the opportunities to use them where You've called me today. Help me to see my work as an extension of my worship, offering it back to You with excellence and purpose. Open my eyes to the moments where I can bring Your light into the lives of those around me, even in the most ordinary tasks. Let my creativity and leadership be a reflection of Your character, and may everything I do bring glory to Your name. In Jesus' name, Amen.

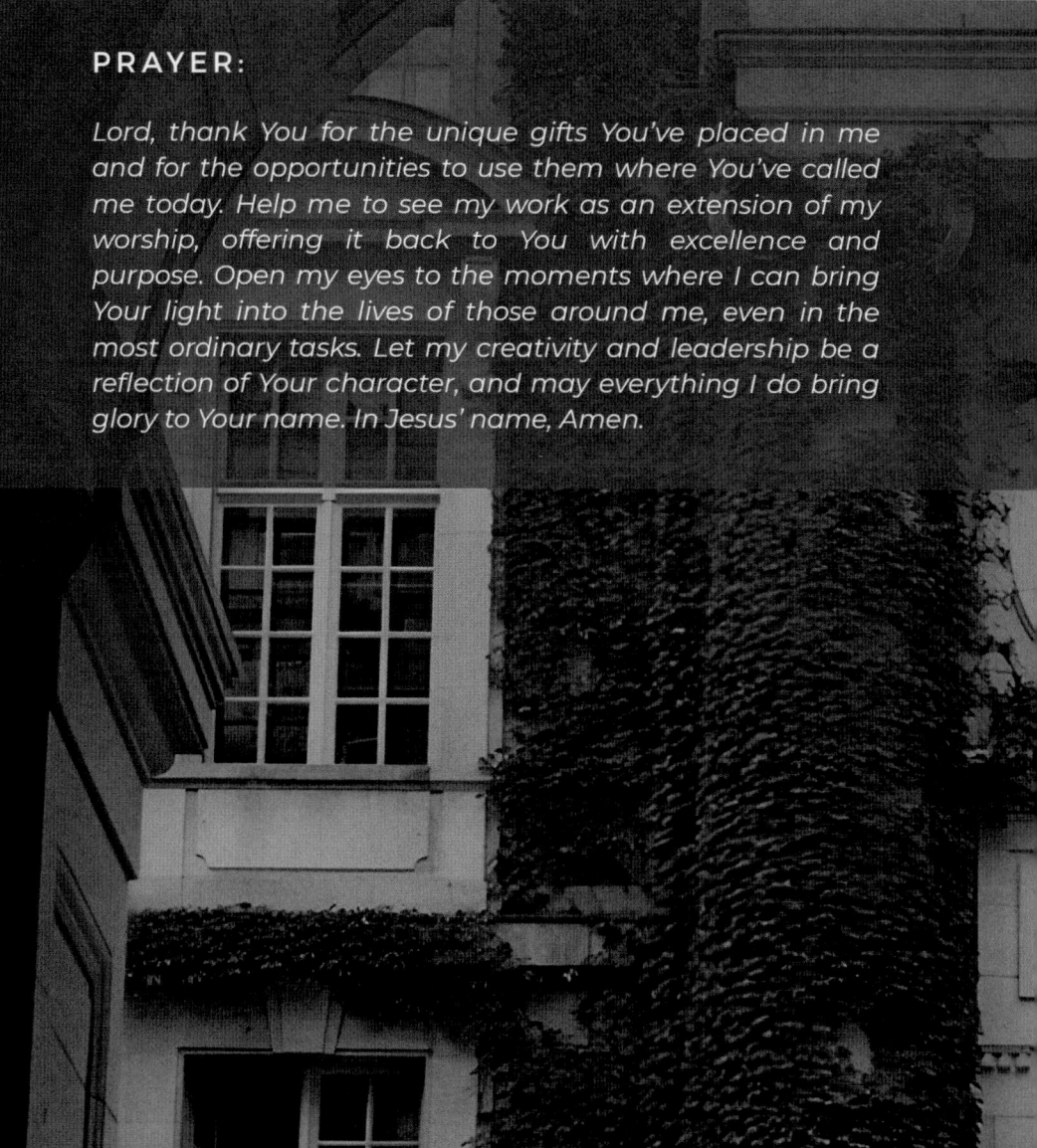

DAY EIGHTEEN

GOD OF ORDER

> **SCRIPTURE:**
>
> *There is a season (a time appointed) for everything and a time for every delight and event or purpose under heaven...*
> —Ecclesiastes 3:1 AMP

For many of us, life feels like a browser with too many tabs open. We rapidly switch between the demands of our work, the needs of our families, and the quiet tug of our own dreams. The transition isn't smooth; it's frantic. And in the rush to respond to everything, the idea of *"balance"* feels like an illusion, slipping through our fingers no matter how hard we try to optimize our calendars.

But what if we're looking for stability in all the wrong places?

In a culture where busyness feels like the only constant, true peace and order can seem like distant dreams. And yet, God, in His goodness, has called us to embrace a divine rhythm—His perfect design for peace and effectiveness.

There's a certain strength in God's order. A peace that settles deep in our souls when we align our lives with His priorities.

Underneath all the rushing and striving, there's a God-given longing within us for something more sustainable. It's a pull towards peace, towards harmony, towards an order that just feels... right. This longing for stability is actually a call to follow God's pattern—a life marked by His priorities, not just our deadlines.

And one of the most significant parts of that pattern is putting people above production.

In our hustle-driven culture, we're taught that to succeed, we must be "always on"—reachable, responsive, and constantly producing.

I know this trap well. There was a season when I poured myself into a new business, convinced that if I just worked harder, responded faster, and showed up at all hours of the day and night, then success would surely follow. But in giving my all to the work, I started to notice something was slipping—precious moments with family, the joy of being fully present, the irreplace-able memories being sacrificed on the altar of productivity. I knew the system was broken.

I started to notice something was slipping—precious moments with family, the joy of being fully present, the irreplaceable memories being sacrificed on the altar of productivity.

This isn't just a personal struggle; it's a *universal* one. It's easy to fall into the mindset that setting boundaries portrays us as uncommitted or weak. But what if setting boundaries is actually a bold act of faith? What if unplugging to honor your family and your health is actually a sign of strength and wisdom, as we trust God to take care of the details?

Stepping back from the constant demand for availability and choosing to be fully present with those closest to us is an act of stewardship. It's a choice to honor the relationships God has entrusted to us. It's a declaration that you believe God's design for order is superior to your need to achieve.

Stepping back from the constant demand for availability and choosing to be fully present with those closest to us is an act of stewardship. It's a choice to honor the relationships God has entrusted to us.

GOD OF ORDER

Our verse today reminds us that God has already appointed seasons and rhythms for every part of our lives. We don't have to force or control what only He can order. Instead, we're invited to step into the right season at the right time, trusting that His design protects what matters most.

Whether in your business operations, your leadership style, or your home life, chaos is not a fruit of the Spirit.

When we surrender our schedules to Him, we discover the freedom of living with peace that settles deep within us, bringing clarity to our decision-making and rest to our souls. It is where both our work and our relationships can flourish under His care.

So as we walk through our own seasons of high demand, let's commit to holding fast to the order that God has set.

You don't have to sacrifice what matters most in the pursuit of success. The Lord can instantly redeem any "lost opportunity" you fear you might miss by stepping back.

It may not always be easy to close the laptop or ignore the phone, but as we relinquish control, a beautiful thing happens: we open ourselves up to the blessings, freedom, and the peace He's been waiting to pour out.

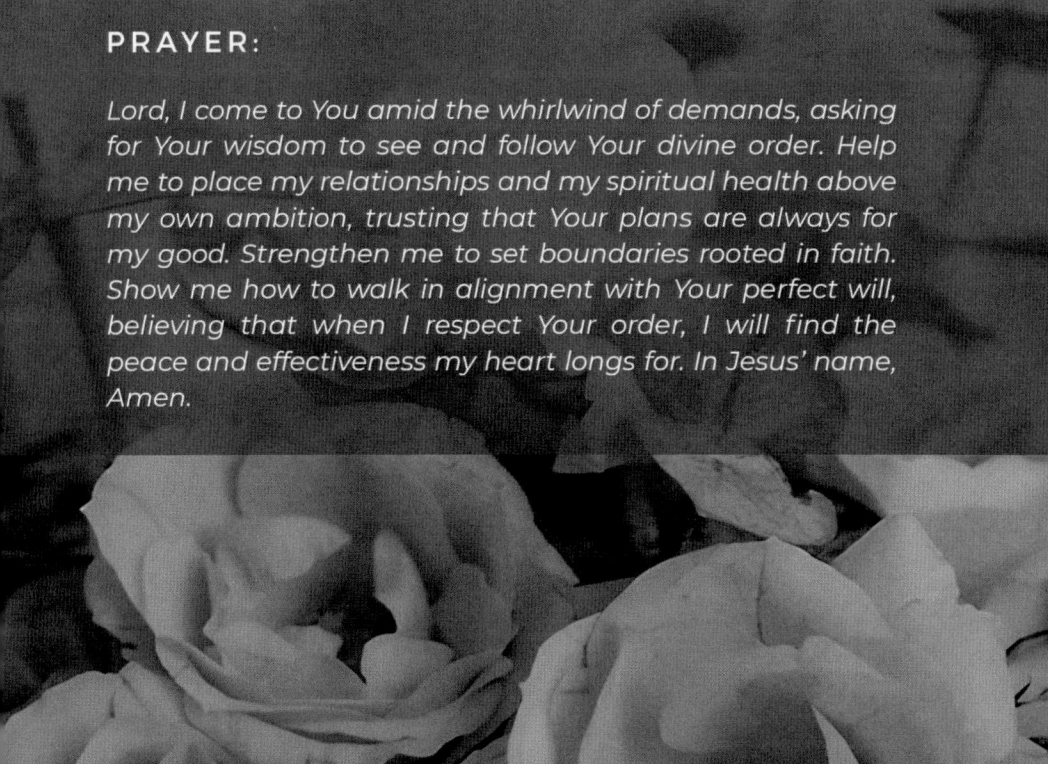

PRAYER:

Lord, I come to You amid the whirlwind of demands, asking for Your wisdom to see and follow Your divine order. Help me to place my relationships and my spiritual health above my own ambition, trusting that Your plans are always for my good. Strengthen me to set boundaries rooted in faith. Show me how to walk in alignment with Your perfect will, believing that when I respect Your order, I will find the peace and effectiveness my heart longs for. In Jesus' name, Amen.

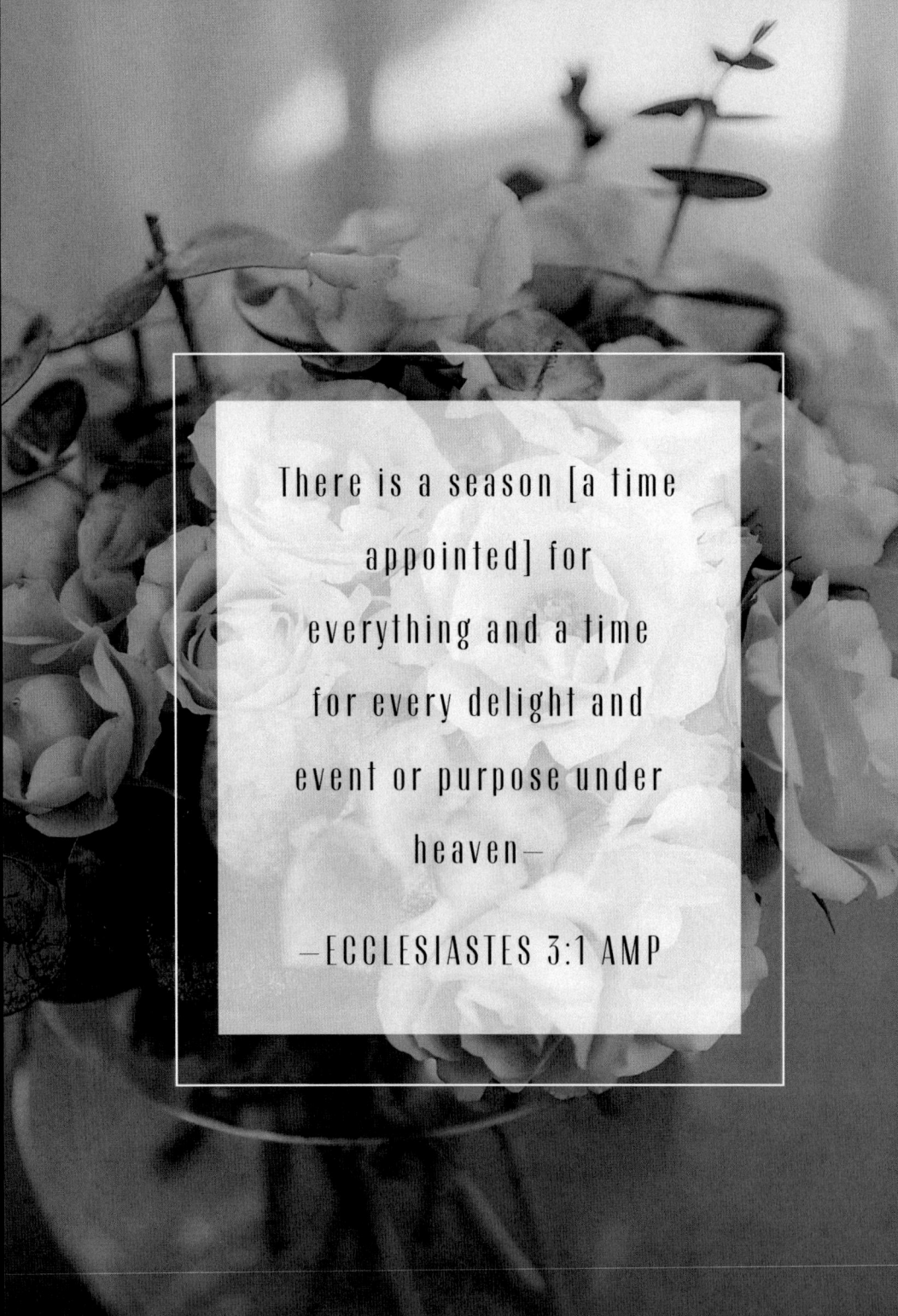

DAY NINETEEN

A JAR OF OIL

19

> **SCRIPTURE:**
>
> *Elisha said to her, "What shall I do for you? Tell me, what do you have [of value] in the house?" She said, "Your maidservant has nothing in the house except a [small] jar of [olive] oil.*
> *—2 King 4:2 (Full Read: 2 Kings 4:1-7)*

Imagine you're sitting at your desk, staring at the new logo you created for a client before shutting the laptop. Or maybe you're standing at your kitchen counter, wiping the remnants of flour from your hands after baking a loaf of sourdough. These small, everyday moments might seem ordinary, but what if they aren't? What if these are the places where your light is meant to shine the brightest?

It's easy to downplay our gifts. When we receive compliments, most of us instinctively shrug them off with phrases like, *"Oh, it's nothing,"* or *"I was just doing my job."* But this habit of apologetic celebration—of diminishing our output—devalues the gift God has placed inside us.

It's time to stop minimizing our contributions.

Neither self-depreciation nor pride serves us well. And your thing—whether it's baking, designing, strategizing, or creating—is not insignificant. It's a resource entrusted to you by God, and He has a purpose for it.

Just like the widow in 2 Kings 4, you may feel like what you have to offer is too small or unremarkable, but we serve a God who specializes in taking what seems small and multiplying it for His glory.

When Elisha asked the widow what she had, her reply was tinged with doubt: *"Nothing...except a small jar of oil."* That oil felt insignificant to her yet, in God's hands, it became a source of abundance—not only saving her family from debt but impacting her community.

Your gifts are like that jar of oil. When poured out in faith, they do not run dry because God is the source of your capability. As you give, He multiplies. The solution you provide, the product you create, or the team you lead may be the blessing someone else has been praying for—a tangible reminder of God's provision and excellence.

Your gifts are like that jar of oil. When poured out in faith, they do not run dry because God is the source of your capability. As you give, He multiplies.

When you trust Him with your gifts, you aren't "just doing a job," or "just serving;" you're participating in a much bigger story. And when you steward your gifts with boldness, you become a leader—a vessel of transformation. Your stewardship, no matter how small it may seem at the start, could inspire someone else to take that brave first step toward their own calling. You never know who is watching you, who is waiting for your courage to spark their own.

Your skills are more than mere talents; they reflect the nature of the Creator who gave them to you. When you use those gifts to serve, you turn your work into an offering—a visible declaration that you are stewarding God's grace to bless others.

So, what does that look like for you? Maybe it means offering your expertise to someone who needs mentorship, or launching something new, not only to turn a profit, but as an act of trust in the Lord's provision.

Each of us has been intentionally crafted by God, equipped with unique talents that are meant to stand out, and there's a whole world out there that needs what you have to offer.

Whatever it is, let your gifts shine, not for applause or recognition, but so that others might see the goodness of God through the work of your hands. When you choose to pour out the gifts you've been given, the world doesn't just get more of you—*it gets more of Him.*

A JAR OF OIL

When you choose to pour out the gifts you've been given, the world doesn't just get more of you—it gets more of Him.

PRAYER:

Thank You for the gifts You've given me. Help me to stop doubting their worth and trust that You can use even the smallest offering for Your glory. Multiply my efforts to bless others and show Your love through everything I do. May my work reflect Your goodness. Thank you, Lord. In Jesus' name, Amen.

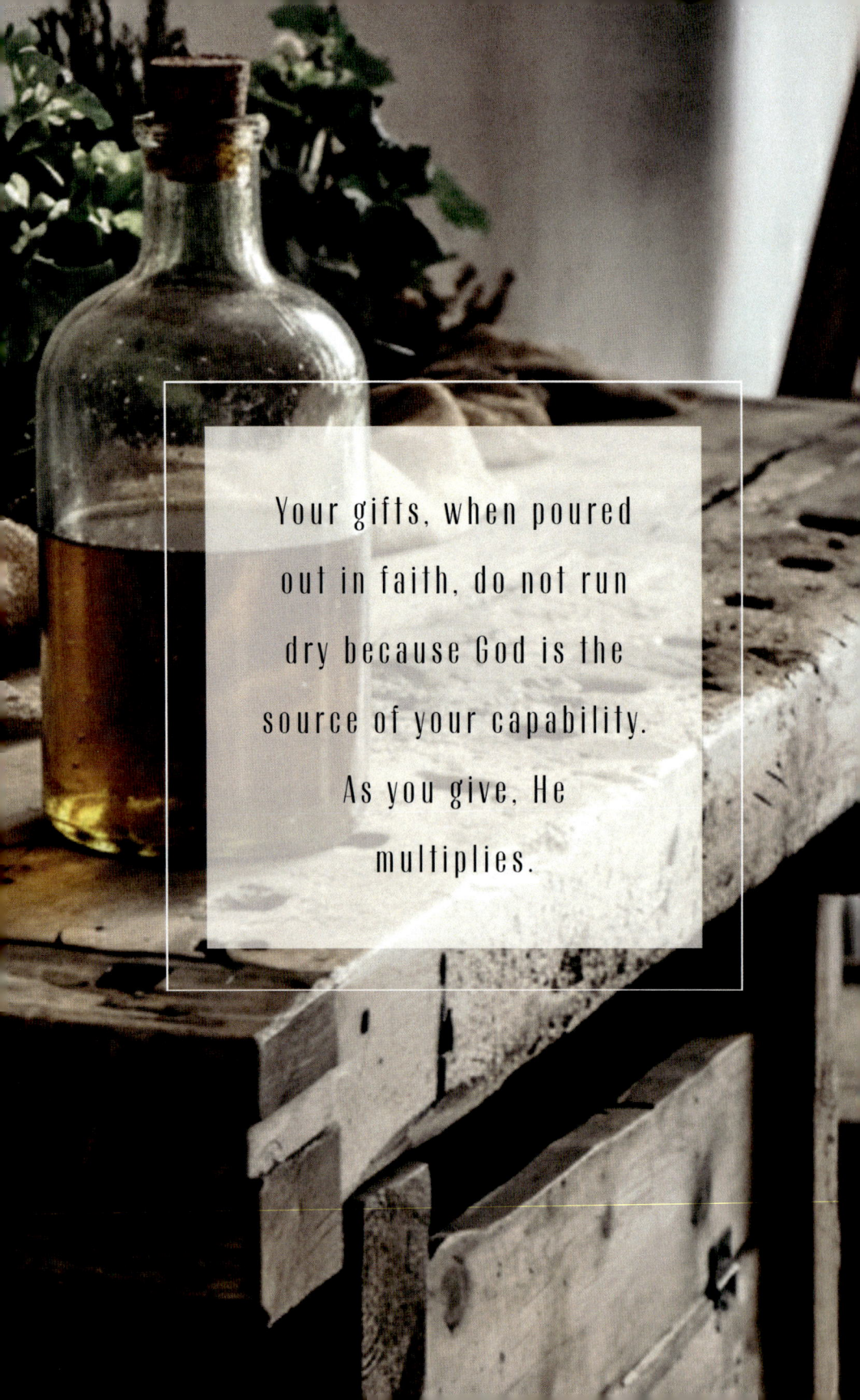

Your gifts, when poured out in faith, do not run dry because God is the source of your capability. As you give, He multiplies.

DAY TWENTY

OVERCOMING FEAR

20

SCRIPTURE:

"Lord, if it's you," Peter replied, "tell me to come to you on the water."

"Come," he said.

Then Peter got down out of the boat, walked on the water and came toward Jesus.

But when he saw the wind, he was afraid and, beginning to sink, cried out, "Lord, save me!"

Immediately Jesus reached out his hand and caught him.
—Matthew 14:28-31

There are times in life when fear feels overwhelming. Think back to the things that scared you as a child—the dark, the crack of thunder, or maybe escalators that seemed to move too fast for your small feet. I can still recall the nerves, the slight panic, at the sight of those moving stair teeth. *What if my shoelace gets caught? What if I mistime my step and trip?*

Fear distorts reality. What we can't yet see or control grows wildly in our minds, turning opportunities into exaggerated obstacles. Even as adults, fear is quick to pull us down. Stepping into an unfamiliar task, sharing something publicly for the first time, or pitching a vision to donors or investors can bring up those same deep-rooted anxieties.

In Scripture, we see a powerful moment of boldness from Peter—a leap of faith that brought him face-to-face with great fear. Imagine the scene: the darkness of the waves, the fierce wind pounding against the boat. The disciples were terrified as they watched what looked like a ghost walking toward them across the stormy lake.

But when Peter hears Jesus' voice, something in him awakens. With a courage born from faith, he asks to do the impossible: to walk on the water.

Jesus replies with a simple, profound invitation: *"Come."*

Peter steps out of the boat—leaving the safety of the known—and for a moment, he defies the laws of nature. Courage floods his heart as his feet meet the water. But as he shifts his gaze from Jesus to the raging waves around him, he analyzes the circumstances. Fear tightens its grip, and he begins to sink.

We do the same, don't we? One moment, we're standing strong in our calling, and then, with a subtle shift of focus—looking at the competition, the economy, or the critics—doubt pulls us under.

Fear is a natural human response, but it becomes problematic when it keeps us from obeying the Lord.

The good news? We aren't expected to walk on water in our own strength. When Peter sank, he didn't need "grit" or "internal courage"—he needed a *Savior*.

And just as Jesus caught Peter, He is right there to catch you. The solution isn't to tread water or muscle through the fear; it's to reach out.

In Scripture, the greatest acts of faith rarely come from calm, controlled settings. Instead, faith often takes root and grows strongest in desperate, unpredictable moments where only God can steady us.

In Scripture, the greatest acts of faith rarely come from calm, controlled settings. Faith often takes root and grows strongest in desperate, unpredictable moments where only God can steady us.

It wasn't cold logic that compelled Moses to face Pharaoh or raise his staff over the Red Sea, nor was it safe calculation that led David to fling a stone at a giant. These weren't fearless men; they were believers acting in deep vulnerability and obedience despite the odds. Sometimes, our most meaningful work is born in a season of desperation.

Each of these Biblical figures was driven by a divine nudge, a call that pushed them past fear and into a purpose far beyond their own strength. That's where deeper faith is born—right there, in the quiet courage of obedience, even when we're afraid.

God often puts dreams in our hearts that are far beyond our own ability or resources. So that sense of inadequacy you feel isn't necessarily a warning to retreat. It may be a divine invitation to rely on Him. Sometimes His plans are so great that the outcome can only bring glory to Him as we recognize our utter dependence on His power.

If there's a dream He's put in your heart—a project, a passion, an idea for Kingdom impact—lean in. Don't wait to feel fearless or ready.

Just as Peter took that bold step out of the boat, God invites us to step beyond what feels comfortable and familiar. The boat represents safety, but it can also represent stagnation if we aren't careful. You can't walk on water if you refuse to get your feet wet.

Faith strengthens as we let go of control and lock eyes with our Savior. And the beautiful part is that He doesn't leave us to face our fears alone. He is with us, equipping us with His presence and guiding us in every step. Fear isn't a disqualifier; it's simply part of the journey.

When God plants His vision in your heart, He's already prepared the provision—whether it's the resources, the people, or the resilience He knows you'll need along the way. You simply have to take the first step.

If you doubt He will show up, look back at your track record of God's faithfulness. That's the confidence you carry into today's challenges and tomorrow's opportunities. Sometimes, God's greatest blessings are found just beyond a step of faith. Don't let fear steal the impact God has planned for your obedience.

Like Peter, we may have moments where we start to sink. But Jesus is always right there, reaching out, ready to lift us up. We only need to keep our focus on Him.

ENTRUSTED

Lean into the faith God is growing in you. Take the next step forward, and as you keep your eyes on Him, He will establish your steps, one by one.

Don't let fear steal the impact God has planned for your obedience.

PRAYER:

Lord, I don't want fear to dictate my steps. I know You've called me to trust You, even when the path feels uncertain. Give me the courage to step out of the boat of comfort and into the waters of obedience. Keep my eyes fixed on You, not the waves. When doubt creeps in, remind me that You are near, ready to catch me if I start to sink. Strengthen my faith, Lord, and help me to walk boldly in the calling You've placed on my life. In Jesus' name, Amen.

DAY TWENTY-ONE

SUCCESS IS OBEDIENCE

SCRIPTURE:

Do not despise these small beginnings, for the Lord rejoices to see the work begin. —Zechariah 4:10 NLT

Have you ever carried the quiet belief that God has something big planned for your life—something beyond the mundane that is meaningful and world-changing?

From a young age, I've felt the weight of that desire. A yearning to do something extraordinary for the Lord, and to be used in a way that leaves a legacy that outlasts my time here. But I've realized that in God's eyes, *every act of obedience is big*. So, even if my life unfolds as a series of small, faithful contributions, each step taken in service to the Lord holds eternal significance, no matter the scale.

> *Even if my life unfolds as a series of small, faithful contributions, each step taken in service to the Lord holds eternal significance, no matter the scale.*

As leaders and doers, the drive to be "successful" by the world's standards can be a constant hum in the background of everything we do. Bigger, faster, more—these expectations often become our markers of worth. But the Lord's view is different.

In our Scripture today, God reassures us with a simple truth: His delight is in the work itself—in the steps of faith we take to begin—no matter how small the start looks.

God's definition of success *is* obedience. Don't aim for "big"; aim for obedient.

The Israelites in Zechariah's time faced a similar tension. They had returned from exile and were rebuilding the temple—a massive construction project—but it seemed small and unimpressive compared to the glory of Solomon's temple. And so, they were tempted to view it as insignificant.

Yet God rejoiced not in the temple's grandeur, but in the heart of obedience that began the work. It wasn't by might or by power, but by His Spirit that the work would be completed (Zechariah 4:6).

While the world applauds results, God celebrates the faith it takes to begin, and to continue, even when the outcome is unseen.

While the world applauds results, God celebrates the faith it takes to begin, and to continue, even when the outcome is unseen.

This principle is just as relevant for us today. Whether you're stepping onto a stage or serving in a role that feels "behind the scenes," the size or worldly impact of your effort does not determine its value. What matters is the obedience behind the work.

Our culture loves a good rags-to-riches story. We idolize the 'self-made' success who pulled themselves up by their bootstraps. But there is a hidden danger in that narrative that tricks us into thinking we are the source of our success, rather than the stewards of God's provision. We forget that it was God who gave the breath, the talent, and the opportunity in the first place.

When we operate from a place of secure identity rather than striving, the goal shifts. We stop asking, *"How can I make this bigger to prove my worth?"* and start asking, *"How can I be faithful with what is in my hands?"*

And yet, faithfulness is rarely glamorous. It usually looks like a long string of ordinary days where nothing spectacular seems to be happening. When the initial adrenaline of a new vision fades, and the visible results are scarce, it is easy to despise the smallness of our work and wonder if it matters at all.

But, like a mustard seed—small, overlooked, and easily dismissed—it grows into a large tree-like structure, strong and deeply rooted. God knows how vital these beginning steps are. These are the moments where we learn, develop humility, and grow our reliance on Him.

In God's economy, small, faithful steps are building blocks for greater things. And while it's okay to dream big, we must hold our plans loosely, letting God guide, shape, and even redirect them. He's more interested in our character—in how we grow through the process—than in the final outcome. This slower pace leaves room for discernment, seeking His will over our own, and developing a heart of stewardship pleasing to Him.

Success may look different from what you expect, and it may come in a smaller package than you planned. But when we view our work through the lens of stewardship, the metric changes. We realize that every effort, every task, and every moment of faithfulness is a victory because it is an offering back to the One who entrusted it to us.

Friends, let us remember that our calling is not to build an empire, but to steward a gift. God has already equipped you with everything you need to do His will—in His way and in His time.

So, release the pressure to measure up. Embrace the freedom that comes from knowing the results aren't on your shoulders. Your job is simply to obey; the outcome belongs to the Lord.

...every effort, every task, and every moment of faithfulness is a victory because it is an offering back to the One who entrusted it to us.

ENTRUSTED

PRAYER:

Lord, I come to You with a heart that often longs for bigger things, but today I'm reminded that You don't measure success the way the world does. Forgive me for the times I've let comparison and striving for "more" overshadow the beauty of simply following where You lead. Help me rest in the truth that obedience is enough, even when it feels small or unseen. Teach my heart to be content in all circumstances, no matter the scale. Shape me, Lord, into a leader who finds peace in obedience. In Jesus' name, Amen.

DAY TWENTY-TWO

FREE FROM YESTERDAY

> **SCRIPTURE:**
>
> Forget about what's happened; don't keep going over old history. Be alert, be present. I'm about to do something brand-new. It's bursting out! Don't you see it? There it is! I'm making a road through the desert, rivers in the badlands. —Isaiah 43:18-19 MSG

ARE YOU LETTING YOUR PAST PAIN SHAPE YOUR FUTURE?

Perhaps you come from a background marked by hardship, trauma, or significant loss. Maybe the remnants of a toxic partnership or deeply hurtful personal chapter still linger, creeping into your thoughts when you least expect them.

Without realizing it, you may be measuring your potential by the pain of your history.

We all have *something*—a chapter we wish we could erase, an event that whispers lies about our competence or worth. For me, abuse, rejection, and neglect had imprinted themselves on my story at a young age. For a time, it felt like a heavy cloak I wore everywhere I went. It covered me, and yet, I always felt exposed, like every stranger somehow *knew* my pain.

I realized I had to find a way to make peace with a past that was trying to define me. Thankfully, God's truth rewrote the narrative: *"Your past is a chapter, not the whole story. Watch. I am doing something new."*

Besides, if the enemy had his way for the first decade of my life, why would I allow him to steal any more time than that?

COULD YESTERDAY'S PAIN BE BLOCKING TODAY'S BLESSINGS?

Here's the reality: You cannot compartmentalize your well-being. We may think we can neatly tuck away our wounds, keeping them separate from our work. But the truth is, unresolved pain has a way of seeping into every corner of our lives.

The burdens we carry become so familiar we don't even notice how they're shaping our days—weaving themselves into our work, our relationships, and even our worship. If we're not careful, unhealed hurt becomes the lens through which we view everything, distorting our perspective and limiting the fullness of what God wants to do in and through us.

Have you ever tried to catch something while holding onto something else? You can't. And yet, so many of us try to step into new seasons while still gripping our old baggage.

We show up in our work carrying the weight of rejection, and suddenly, every bit of constructive feedback feels like a personal attack. We engage in friendships, but an old betrayal whispers, *"Don't trust too much."* We stand in church, hands lifted, yet our hearts stay clenched because we're still wondering if God is as good as He says He is.

Sometimes we grip pain so tightly, thinking it protects us when it's the very thing that's keeping us stuck. But holding on to bitterness, pain, or regret doesn't just keep us from healing—it keeps us from *receiving*.

Holding on to bitterness, pain, or regret doesn't just keep us from healing—it keeps us from receiving.

HEALING IS A CHOICE

It's easy to convince ourselves that some wounds are best left buried—that if we push them down far enough, time will do the hard work of healing for us. But we can't expect a harvest of joy when we still have buried seeds of unresolved pain.

Buried things don't simply go away. They take root under the surface, in the dark, growing in ways we don't expect. Before long, what we thought was forgotten is shaping our perspective and actions.

What if the very things we refuse to release are the barriers preventing us from experiencing God's best?

Once we release the pain that has weighed us down, we make room for the vision and assignment God has planted within us. We clear the runway for His new mercies and the incredible blessings He is pouring out. The freedom, the purpose, and the assignment He's prepared for us—it's all waiting. But our hands have to be open to receive it.

God can't heal what we refuse to bring into the light. So maybe today, it's time to name what you've buried. Dig it up and lay it at the feet of Jesus—letting Him do what only He can do: bring light, healing, and freedom.

His desire is for you to live fully free—not just surviving your past. But healing is not a passive process; it's a choice, a daily decision to surrender. The Lord doesn't promise it will be easy, but He does promise His presence in the process.

Healing is not a passive process; it's a choice, a daily decision to surrender.

Scripture reminds us that even our hardest moments can serve a greater purpose when surrendered to God. We are promised that *"in all things, He works for the good of those who love Him"* (Romans 8:28).

This means our trials can transform into testimonies. In fact, it's often through our pain that God plants the seeds of our greatest empathy and impact.

When you allow the Lord into every part of your story, He brings healing that overflows into every area of your life. God's not only interested in fixing what's broken; He's preparing you for something new. When you release the weight of the past, you open yourself to the fullness of what He's doing in your present.

Often, it's through our pain that God plants the seeds of our greatest empathy and impact.

WHAT DO YOU NEED TO RELEASE TODAY?

I don't know your story, but I do know pain is easy to find in this life. Maybe you're walking through a crisis right now, or perhaps you've just come out of a season that nearly broke you. Or, without realizing it, you've been carrying the weight of something for years, tucking it away, convincing yourself it doesn't still affect you—until it does.

The reality is, hurt is a universal language—*but so is redemption.* If we let Him, God can take even our deepest wounds and turn them into powerful examples of His healing.

*Hurt is a universal language—**but so is redemption.***

IS THERE A PAST HURT GOD IS ASKING YOU TO EXCHANGE FOR FREEDOM TODAY?

The Lord wants to make a way in your wilderness, to bring streams to your present. Don't let the past hold you back from an opportunity for renewal.

What happened to you doesn't define you; it refines you. Know that once you commit to continually surrendering your past to God, it no longer holds power over your story. Step into the future He is preparing. Your past pain is a testimony of how far God has carried you.

FREE FROM YESTERDAY

PRAYER:

Heavenly Father, thank You for reminding me that I am not defined by the struggles or failures of my past. Help me release what no longer serves me and open my heart to the healing You have prepared. Show me how to let go of resentment and embrace the future with courage. I long to bear fruit that reflects Your goodness and blesses those around me. Thank You that my identity lies not in what has been done to me, but in what has been done for me by Christ. In Jesus' name, Amen.

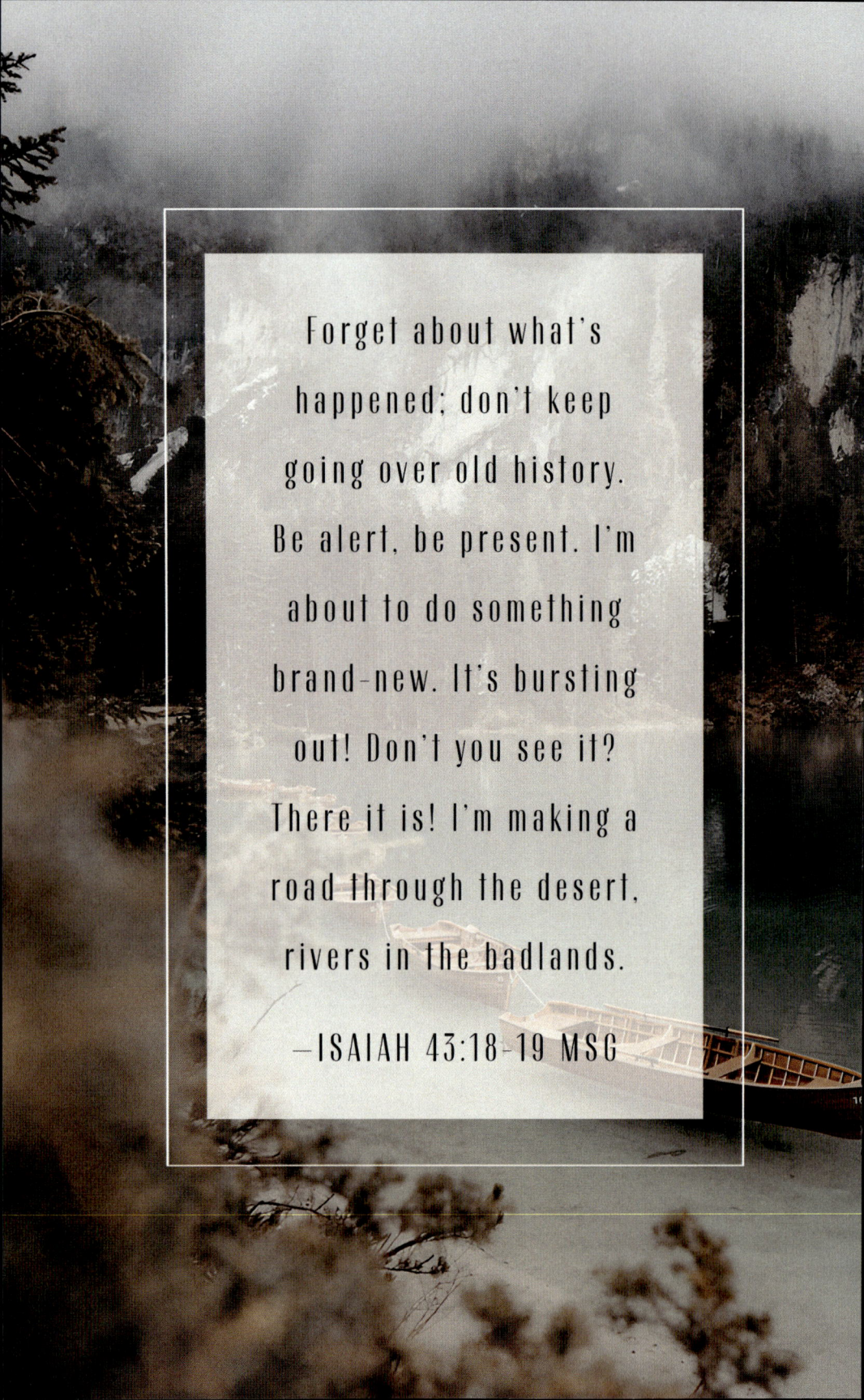

> Forget about what's happened; don't keep going over old history. Be alert, be present. I'm about to do something brand-new. It's bursting out! Don't you see it? There it is! I'm making a road through the desert, rivers in the badlands.
>
> —ISAIAH 43:18-19 MSG

DAY TWENTY-THREE

INDECISION

> **SCRIPTURE:**
>
> *And we know [with great confidence] that God [who is deeply concerned about us] causes all things to work together [as a plan] for good for those who love God, to those who are called according to His plan and purpose.* —Romans 8:28 AMP

Analysis paralysis is the enemy of momentum.

It masquerades as wisdom—telling us we need to do "a little more research" or "pray about it one more time." But often, it is fear dressed up as prudence.

You sense the invitation to move, but you find yourself caught in a loop of overthinking. The clarity you crave remains out of reach. The weight of uncertainty and the fear of "getting it wrong" stalls your progress.

What you really want is a guarantee—a clear roadmap so you can move forward without hesitation.

If you're anything like me, saying "yes" to God isn't hard—it's the action that follows. It's the leap of faith where the stakes feel high. *What if I choose the wrong thing? What if this leads to failure? What if I miss God's will?*

Indecision is one of the enemy's most effective tactics to stall your impact. Recall the old leadership adage: You can't steer a parked car. We often disguise our hesitation as "waiting on the Lord," but sometimes it's simply a way to avoid the risk of moving forward. The enemy knows that if he can keep you lingering at the crossroads, distracted with endless options, he doesn't need to stop you; you will stop yourself.

Indecision becomes a decision—a decision to stay stuck.

I've been there. Agonizing over decisions, afraid that one wrong move could take me off the path God intends for my life. In those high-stakes moments, it's easy to get lost in the belief that success only comes through the "right" choice, and that failure is the guaranteed result of making the "wrong" one.

But our God is so much bigger than that!

Success isn't defined by a particular path. It's defined by a heart surrendered to God. His promises aren't contingent on your ability to make flawless choices; they're upheld by His goodness and faithfulness.

If you desire to honor God and steward your life for His glory, you can step forward knowing that even if you misstep, it isn't the end of His plan.

Success isn't defined by a particular path. It's defined by a heart surrendered to God. His promises aren't contingent on your ability to make flawless choices; they're upheld by His goodness, and faithfulness.

That's the freedom we have in Christ—not the pressure to never miss the mark, but the assurance that God is always at work, guiding and redeeming our steps. When our hearts are set on honoring Him, we can move forward in faith, trusting that He is bigger than our uncertainties.

Yes, there is a time to wait on God. But let's be discerning about whether our waiting is truly seeking Him or simply avoiding action. If you find yourself waiting simply because the next step feels overwhelming, or you're afraid of the risk, then that's not wisdom—that's fear keeping you stagnant. Faith requires movement.

If you feel paralyzed by chaos, remember that *that* is not from God (1 Corinthians 14:33). However, do not mistake a lack of details for chaos. God often gives us peace without giving us the full picture. Total certainty leaves no room for faith. So let's stop waiting for perfect clarity before we dare to move.

INDECISION

Let's be discerning about whether our waiting is truly seeking Him or simply avoiding action. Faith requires movement.

When you start taking steps in faith—even small, imperfect ones, you'll see that God meets you there.

You can step forward knowing that God's grace is greater than your imperfections. As men and women called to use our gifts, we can trust that whichever path we choose, He will work through it all for His glory. In trusting Him, we can finally move forward, free to build, free to explore, free to decide, and free to see His hand work in our lives.

PRAYER:

Father, thank You for the freedom I have in Christ. Help me overcome indecision and the fear of making the wrong choice. Empower me to step out in faith. Remind me that Your promises cover my imperfections. Guide me as I navigate the decisions before me, granting me wisdom to choose in alignment with Your will. I surrender my uncertainty about the future, and I trust that You will guide me as I begin to move. In Jesus' name, amen.

And we know [with great confidence] that God [who is deeply concerned about us] causes all things to work together [as a plan] for good for those who love God, to those who are called according to His plan and purpose.

—ROMANS 8:28 AMP

DAY TWENTY-FOUR

WHEN PRESSURE BRINGS PURPOSE

> **SCRIPTURE:**
>
> *Then I went down to the potter's house, and saw that he was working at the wheel. [4] But the vessel that he was making from clay was spoiled by the potter's hand; so he made it over, reworking it and making it into another pot that seemed good to him. —Jeremiah 18:3-4* AMP

When I think back to my art class in school, I'm reminded of a girl who spent every spare moment at the pottery wheel. You could faintly see her through the shelves of drying pottery in the back corner of the room, where she would sit at a wheel, throwing clay for hours.

It was always messy, but I was so intrigued with how she could gently shape this mud into beautiful, purposeful pieces on a spinning wheel. She wore her clay-streaked apron with pride, lost in her own little world as she molded and shaped. Every time I passed, I was captivated by the beauty of her dedication.

When we read about the Potter and the clay, it's easy to romanticize the image—a quiet workshop, the rhythmic spinning of the wheel, the gentle shaping of a vessel.

But if you're the clay, the process feels anything but gentle.

To be shaped requires friction.

It requires being pressed, pulled, and spun. It means enduring intense pressure from the Potter's hands to align the clay with His design.

We all feel this pressure in our lives. Pride is being pressed out of us. Our control is being pried from our fingers. Our trust is being stretched beyond what feels comfortable.

We feel the disorientation of the spin and the heat of the kiln. In those moments, we often ask, *"Lord, why is this so hard? Why is there so much resistance?"*

Changing the shape of your character is never easy or free of pain, but it's a beautiful pain—a purposeful pressing. God's plan is always to shape the vessel into something useful for His Kingdom and pleasing to Him.

Changing the shape of your character is never easy or free of pain, but it's a beautiful pain—a purposeful pressing.

Jeremiah's vision of the Potter is a vivid reminder that God is fully aware of the clay's imperfections. It offers a profound encouragement for anyone who feels they have messed up or "spoiled" their opportunity.

The Scripture describes the vessel becoming marred *by* the Potter's hand. In pottery, this happens not because the Master made a mistake, but because the clay resisted the shaping or held a hidden impurity that couldn't withstand the pressure.

Maybe you feel like that today. Maybe a lapse in integrity, a failed audition, or a personal setback has revealed a flaw in your own foundation, leaving you feeling marred or broken—like you have missed your chance to be used by God.

But notice the Potter's reaction. He doesn't toss the clay into the scrap pile. He doesn't walk away in frustration. He reworks it.

He gathers the clay back up and begins shaping it again to build something more true to His original design. He uses the same material to create a new vessel.

Think of the Potter's wheel as the constant swirl of circumstances in your life. God's foot presses the pedal, determining the speed, the spin, and the rhythm. His hands work the clay, just as the Holy Spirit works in us. When the Potter puts a precise amount of pressure on the clay, and it accepts the transformation under His hand, the pressure is relieved. He relents, pulling away. He knows the exact amount of pressure needed to correct our shape and when to ease up, allowing us to rest in the form He's created.

WHEN PRESSURE BRINGS PURPOSE

There's pressure, but there's also release. And when we yield to the Potter's hands—allowing Him to reshape our character and realign our ambitions—we become vessels He's proud to display.

It's easy to feel like we're just marred clay—that maybe we don't have anything special to offer. But what if you're simply in the midst of transformation? What if God is preparing you, right now, for a purpose beyond what you can imagine?

Wait with hope. The enemy wants you to believe that your imperfections disqualify you. But the Potter knows exactly what He is making, even if it feels a little wobbly. He sees the finished product before He even sits at the wheel.

He knew you before you were born (Jeremiah 1:5).

He knows the plans He has for you (Jeremiah 29:11).

And if you look at a masterpiece of pottery, you will see a small detail that makes it valuable: it is signed by its maker.

Your Creator has marked you.

You're not significant because of what you do. You are significant because of Who made you.

Your Creator has marked you. You're not significant because of what you do. You are significant because of Who made you.

But He also didn't create you to sit on a shelf. He crafted you with a specific intent—to be an instrument in His hands.

2 Timothy 2:21 AMP says, *"Therefore, if anyone cleanses himself from these things [which are dishonorable—disobedient, sinful], he will be a vessel for honor, sanctified [set apart for a special purpose and], useful to the Master, prepared for every good work."*

We've been invited to become vessels of honor in the hands of our Maker. Whether you are in the fire, on the wheel, sitting on a shelf waiting, or feeling dried up, take heart. We are jars of clay, holding treasures the world needs to see, treasures that reflect His

ENTRUSTED

glory through us. Every detail, every redeemed flaw, and every stroke of His hand is creating something resilient in you.

Let's embrace this journey, knowing that we're signed, sealed, and held by our Maker.

We are jars of clay, holding treasures the world needs to see, treasures that reflect His glory through us. Every detail, every redeemed flaw, and every stroke of His hand is creating something resilient in you.

PRAYER:

God, as I consider the molding and forming You're doing in my life, I ask You to have Your way. When the pressure feels intense, remind me that Your hands are always holding and shaping me. Help me to yield, to be still, and to trust the process so I can become all You've designed me to be. I pray that the fires in my life will strengthen me, readying me to do Your work. Thank You for making me unique, purposeful, and a vessel for Your glory. In Jesus' name, Amen.

DAY TWENTY-FIVE

NO HOLINESS IN STRUGGLE

25

> **SCRIPTURE:**
>
> *But you shall remember [with profound respect] the Lord your God, for it is He who is giving you power to make wealth, that He may confirm His covenant which He swore (solemnly promised) to your fathers, as it is this day.* —Deuteronomy 8:18 AMP

Do you ever feel uneasy about making money? Maybe you've heard, *"Money is the root of all evil,"* so many times it's hard to imagine wealth as anything but a temptation. Or perhaps you grew up struggling, so your family was quick to criticize the wealthy. Perhaps you have a subconscious belief that *wealthy people are a certain type* of person—different from you. But wealth isn't the problem—our mindset about it is.

Deuteronomy 8:18 reminds us that the power to create wealth is a gracious gift from God. As Moses prepared the Israelites to enter the Promised Land, he taught them that their success was not born of their own hustle, but flowed from God's faithful provision.

In the same way, we are called to remember that true success isn't rooted in self-reliance; rather, it is God who gives us the ability to create wealth for his purposes.

When we're faithful in managing what He gives, we see that it's not only okay to prosper—it's often His design for us to do so. While this isn't a guarantee of luxury, it's a promise that God will supply what we need to carry out our assignment. Poverty does not glorify God if it prevents you from doing His will.

Here's the truth every Kingdom leader needs to grasp: *There is no holiness in struggle.*

There is no holiness in struggle.

Financial hardship doesn't make anyone more holy. It makes them broke. But for many of us, the thought of succeeding financially stirs up feelings of guilt or discomfort.

I get it. When I opened my first business, I felt deeply uncomfortable with the concept of charging for my work. Every time I priced an item or sent an invoice, guilt would creep in, whispering doubts about whether my work was truly worth the cost.

But it wasn't my place to decide the value based on my insecurity; the market decides the value based on the solution provided.

Maybe you can relate. Do you find yourself undervaluing your time, your products, or your services—believing it's more "godly" to charge less?

Playing small might feel humble or easier in the moment, but it won't cover your expenses. Running a business or leading an organization means acknowledging that making money isn't just okay—it's *essential*. If you aren't profitable, you aren't sustainable. And if you aren't sustainable, you can't serve anyone long-term. After all, if you're not making money, all you have is a hobby.

This truth challenges us to redefine our perspective and embrace financial success as a way to glorify God. Our success isn't a sign of selfishness; it's a reflection of His provision.

If you cling to a poverty mindset, you limit the resources God can entrust to your care. Proverbs 4:24 (MSG) encourages us: *"Don't talk out of both sides of your mouth."* In other words, we can't ask God to bless the work of our hands while simultaneously feeling guilty when revenue comes in.

Money itself is *amoral*—it's a tool. God doesn't care about the number in the bank account; He cares about your motivation and the posture of your heart. Money simply amplifies who we already are. If you are generous, wealth allows you to be more generous. If you are greedy, wealth makes you greedier. Your character remains the same, rich or poor.

Money simply amplifies who we already are—our character remains the same, rich or poor.

It's important to address this misconception clearly: It's not the money itself, it's *"the love of money [that is, the greedy desire for it and the willingness to gain it unethically] is a root of all sorts of evil"* (1 Timothy 6:10, AMP).

When we idolize money or place it above our relationships and faith, then it becomes problematic. But when viewed correctly, it's a tool for meeting needs, funding ministry, and advancing God's purposes.

There is no shortage of resources in God's Kingdom. Your gain does not mean someone else's loss. All money is His—not yours. You are simply the fund manager. So, *steward wisely.*

As you move forward, remember that God's provision isn't something to shy away from—it's something to celebrate. When we shift our perspective, we open the door to greater impact. Keep walking in faith, stewarding His resources with integrity, and embracing His abundant provision with a grateful heart.

There is no shortage of resources in God's Kingdom. Your gain does not mean someone else's loss.

ENTRUSTED

PRAYER:

Lord, I release my fears and misconceptions about money into Your hands. Teach me to see wealth through the lens of Your truth—as a tool to be stewarded for Your glory. Remind me that the power to create wealth comes from You. Align my desires with Yours so that my success reflects Your goodness and funds Your Kingdom. Break any poverty mindset that hinders my stewardship. In Jesus' name, Amen.

DAY TWENTY-SIX

HEDGE OF PROTECTION

> **SCRIPTURE:**
>
> *Have You not put a hedge [of protection] around him and his house and all that he has, on every side? You have blessed the work of his hands [and conferred prosperity and happiness upon him], and his possessions have increased in the land.*
> —Job 1:10 AMP

We all have an innate desire for security. In our personal lives, we lock doors and install alarms. It's why we move to neighborhoods that feel safe or choose schools that promise to protect our kids. In business, we sign contracts, buy insurance, and mitigate risk to protect what we've built. We surround ourselves with layers of security to safeguard what matters most.

But what about the unseen battles? What about the spiritual opposition that's just as real, if not more so, than the tangible dangers we face? So often, we overlook it. We either fail to recognize the depth of the fight we're in, or we're unaware of how fiercely we are being defended.

When I think of spiritual protection, I think of Job. God placed a hedge of protection around him, safeguarding his family, his assets, and his work. Now, if you know the story of Job, I know what you're thinking: *"Job is practically the poster child for loss—how could he have been protected?"* But God's protection isn't always about keeping trouble from reaching us, and just because Job faced large trials doesn't mean he wasn't protected. Stay with me for a moment.

In Biblical times, a *hedge* wasn't ornamental—like the shrubs lining a suburban yard today. It was a dense wall of thornbushes, woven together to form an impenetrable barrier designed to keep wild animals out and what was precious safe within. That's the kind of spiritual protection available to us today as we steward our gifts.

God's blessing over Job was undeniable. His family thrived, his work flourished, and everything he touched seemed to prosper.

And Satan?

He noticed.

He accused Job of being faithful *only* because of his abundance. You see, the enemy doesn't waste time attacking those who aren't a threat to his plans.

Convinced that if Job's blessings disappeared, so would his devotion, the enemy sought permission to test him.

Permission.

Let that sink in. The enemy couldn't lay a finger on Job without God's consent. That means, your life—every trial, every struggle—is under God's authority, not the enemy's. And while God may allow challenges, they are there to shape you. *Nothing—absolutely nothing*—can touch your life unless God allows it. That truth changes everything.

Have you ever noticed that as soon as you step out in faith, resistance shows up? Right on cue. You take a bold step forward, and the pushback feels immediate. The reality is, we face the same enemy today that Job did. His goal is to neutralize the impact of your gifts. He wants to shake your faith and make you question if you're really on the right path.

I used to get flustered when I faced resistance while preparing to lead worship on Sunday mornings—whether it was a last-minute musician calling in sick, technical issues, or another power outage. But when I considered the *spiritual* reality, it changed my perspective. There was a new motivation in realizing I was stepping into battle as I ushered others into the throne room each Sunday morning.

Recognizing that using your God-given gifts is an act of warfare reframes the struggle. Resistance isn't always a sign of failure; sometimes, it's confirmation that you are walking in obedience and that your gifts are making a dent in the darkness.

The enemy doesn't waste time attacking those who aren't a threat to his plans.

HEDGE OF PROTECTION

This brings us to a critical question: How do we actively cultivate this spiritual hedge around our work and calling? While the Word promises that the Lord *"will strengthen you and protect you from the evil one"* (2 Thessalonians 3:3), we must remember that a hedge requires tending. It isn't a passive shield; it is a living barrier that thrives on intentional faith.

HERE ARE FOUR WAYS TO FORTIFY YOUR HEDGE:

1. STAY ROOTED IN PRAYER

Prayer is more than a defense mechanism; it's an active declaration of trust. When you pray over your family, your work, and your calling, you are reinforcing the perimeter of God's covering. Don't wait for the crisis to hit—be proactive. Prayer is the maintenance plan for your protection.

2. SPEAK FAITH, NOT FEAR

Fear creates breaches in the hedge, but faith fortifies it. When the enemy whispers that you aren't enough or that the risk is too high, do not agree with him. Counter the lie with the Word. Your words have the power to dismantle the enemy's accusations before they take root.

3. WORSHIP AS WARFARE

Worship isn't reserved exclusively for Sunday mornings; it's an everyday weapon. Whether you're crunching numbers, building a house, or writing a proposal, doing your work *"as unto the Lord"* shifts the atmosphere. When you turn your workplace into a sanctuary, the enemy has to flee.

4. WALK IN DISCIPLINE & OBEDIENCE

Obedience is the most secure position for a believer. Just as a hole in a fence lets the wild animals in, compromise creates gaps in our spiritual defense. When we align our creative process, our business practices, and our leadership with His Word, we position ourselves safely under His covering.

What strikes me as most profound is the symbolism of the hedge itself. Those same thornbushes, intentionally designed to guard what mattered most in the Old Testament, reappear in the New Testament as a crown of thorns placed on the head of our Savior.

The very thing once meant to protect became a symbol of ultimate sacrifice. A reminder that He stepped into the spiritual battle for us, securing an impenetrable protection we could never build on our own—absorbing the pain, the sin, and the brokenness so that we could stand eternally secure.

What was once a hedge became a crown. What was once for defense became an emblem of love so fierce that it tore through the barrier of death itself.

So when the battle feels intense, and you think the hedge around you is under siege, cling to the reality that the Lord has built your hedge.

Pray fervently. Lead boldly. Steward your gifts fully.

You are not fighting for victory; you're fighting *from* victory. In Him, every thorn, every battle, and every moment of resistance is ordained for your transformation and redeemed for His glory.

PRAYER:

God, thank You for being my refuge and defender. Thank You for the hedge of protection You place around me and the work You have entrusted to me. Help me to be aware of the spiritual battles I face and even more aware of Your mighty hand at work. When battles come, remind me that You are fighting on my behalf. I ask for Your hand of protection over my family, my resources, and my calling. In Jesus' name, Amen.

DAY TWENTY-SEVEN

SACRED SEPARATION

SCRIPTURE:

Then Elijah said to him, "Stay here; the Lord has sent me to the Jordan."

And he replied, "As surely as the Lord lives and as you live, I will not leave you." So the two of them walked on.

Fifty men from the company of the prophets went and stood at a distance, facing the place where Elijah and Elisha had stopped at the Jordan. Elijah took his cloak, rolled it up and struck the water with it. The water divided to the right and to the left, and the two of them crossed over on dry ground. —2 Kings 2: 6-8

Imagine the scene: Elijah and Elisha approach the Jordan River, the air thick with expectation. Along the journey, Elijah had urged Elisha multiple times to stay behind, yet he remained steadfast in his commitment. Now, with fifty observers standing at a distance, Elijah rolls up his cloak, strikes the river, and watches as the waters part before them. Together, they cross over on dry ground. This reveals a timeless truth: God often leads us to places where few will follow.

Sometimes elevation requires separation.

And by elevation, I don't mean the pursuit of personal advancement or God lifting us to a place of prominence; I mean God refining and preparing you for greater responsibility and deeper stewardship in His Kingdom.

Sometimes elevation requires separation.

Though it may be painful, we must acknowledge that not everyone is equipped to accompany us on the unique path God has laid out for our growth, gifts, and Kingdom impact.

As believers, we often find ourselves feeling isolated, especially when pursuing a vision that is deeply personal, God-inspired, and misunderstood by the crowd. In God's design, separation often precedes transformation. It's essential to discern who has the capacity to walk beside us and who is better suited to remain on the shore, watching from a distance.

Reflect on Elijah's intentional actions. He understood the weight of his assignment and fiercely protected it. He didn't plead for company; instead, he tested Elisha's loyalty, filtering out those who couldn't endure the journey.

This discernment is crucial for us, too. As we work to integrate our professional ambitions with our spiritual calling, we may encounter resistance from those around us. Some may view God's plan for you as unsettling to their comfort zones or misunderstand your calling because it doesn't align with their expectations. But obedience to God always surpasses others' expectations.

Obedience to God always surpasses the expectations of others.

Consider Jesus' journey. As He approached the cross, though He called many to follow, His circle narrowed significantly, reflecting the depth of His mission. Many fell away, yet He remained steadfast with those who were committed to His purpose and willing to endure the difficult road with Him.

Similarly, as you grow in your faith, scale your business, or level up your parenting game, your circle may shift. This can feel unsettling at first, but it is also freeing. It allows you to make space for genuine support—people who understand that what you are doing is a reflection of God's work.

As we navigate the intersection of passion and calling, we must accept that not everyone is equipped for where God is taking us. This reality makes the faithful few who walk beside us rare and invaluable treasures.

So, seek out like-minded allies. Look for those who encourage you to follow God's lead—people who see not only where you are now but also the incredible future the Lord has for you. These are the ones who will uplift and sharpen you when the journey feels tough.

So, what distinguishes the true ally from the crowd? It is the hunger for the mission. Consider Elisha.

There is a reason Elisha refused to stay behind. He wasn't just chasing Elijah; he was chasing the anointing that rested on him. He knew that to receive the 'double portion'—the increased capacity for miracles and ministry—he had to be present when the transition happened.

The mantle of leadership is rarely dropped in the crowd; it is passed in the quiet, difficult moments of one-on-one discipleship. If Elisha had stayed with the fifty prophets on the shore, he would have remained a spectator. By crossing the water, he became a successor. The separation wasn't a punishment; it was the prerequisite for what would follow.

In moments of doubt or isolation, remind yourself that the Lord is faithful to guide and support us through each season.

Release those who keep you tethered to past narratives. Trust in God's guidance, knowing that sometimes the very act of stepping forward means leaving behind what hinders the calling. Trust that He is creating space for new connections—ones that will propel you forward into your purpose.

As we stand at the edge of our own Jordans, let's embrace the truth that in the end, our circle may be small, but it is aligned, and exactly what we need for the journey ahead.

Trust in God's guidance, knowing that sometimes the very act of stepping forward means leaving behind what hinders the calling.

ENTRUSTED

PRAYER:

Father, grant me the wisdom to discern which relationships align with Your purpose for my life and my work. Help me to release those who may hinder the assignment You have for me in this season. Give me the courage to forge ahead, even when the path feels lonely. Surround me with like-minded individuals who uplift and encourage me to pursue Your will. Fill my corner with Your presence and the support of those who walk beside me in faith. In Jesus' name, Amen.

DAY TWENTY-EIGHT

UNSETTLED BUT LED

SCRIPTURE:

Your word is a lamp for my feet, a light on my path.
—Psalm 119:105 AMP

Sometimes, we settle into a place of quiet compromise.

Life moves smoothly, predictably—even comfortably—and our souls start to drift into a state of stagnation. We fill our days with tasks that require little faith, little risk, little reliance on God.

And yet, deep within, there's a stirring—a sense that we were made for more. Not more striving or hitting higher targets, but more trust, more impact, more walking by faith than sight.

Could it be that God is gently unsettling us, not to disrupt our peace, but to awaken us to His purpose?

Perhaps it's time to be pulled from the quicksand of compromise that slowly, subtly keeps us from what we're truly called to steward.

We weren't made for stagnant, shallow efforts. God often calls us beyond what feels comfortable or familiar.

He wants us to *crave* righteousness for righteousness' sake, to seek His ways, and follow where He leads—even when the destination isn't clear.

Sometimes, He invites us to step into the unknown, where His light, like a lamp, only illuminates enough of the path to take the next step.

We crave a floodlight. We want the 5-year strategic plan, the complete picture of the destination, and the itinerary of every twist and turn. But God often offers us a soft, subtle glow instead.

HEBREW:

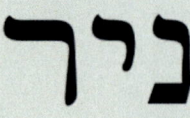

Derived from a root meaning "to glisten," *niyr* refers to a lamp or light—either literal or figurative—symbolizing illumination, guidance, or revelation. It can be translated as lamp, light, or candle in Scripture.[3]

In Psalm 119, the Hebrew word *niyr*, meaning *"lamp,"* refers to the small oil lamps used in Biblical times, casting just enough light to see a small area around one's feet. Travelers then had no floodlights to expose the entire path; instead, they relied on that steady, humble glow to safely walk dark, uneven paths.

We, too, are asked to lean into the next right step rather than demanding to see the whole picture.

Change is rarely comfortable. By nature, we cling to what's known and familiar. But God's purpose is to deepen our character and mold us into His likeness.

His plan for you *is* change—transformation—that not only shifts your actions but reshapes your heart to reflect His.

His plan for you is change—transformation—that not only shifts your actions but reshapes your heart to reflect His.

The unknown looming before you may feel unsettling. We crave security in knowing the outcome. But the Lord promises, *"I will not leave you as orphans... I will come to you"* (John 14:18).

You aren't abandoned in the dark; you are being guided through the shadowed pathways of life.

Maybe you feel called to step into something new—serving on a new team, leading a Bible study, or something that feels beyond your experience. It can be daunting to leave what's known and stretch into the unfamiliar, but God delights in drawing out the gifts He's placed within you.

When you surrender and allow God's Word to guide each step, what's ahead might just become your promised land. This new territory might be where your gifts align with His assignment.

When you surrender and allow God's Word to guide each step, what's ahead might just become your promised land. This new territory might be where your gifts align with His assignment.

So, where are you on this path? Are you following the light of God, allowing Him to lead you through the unknown, or are you clutching at the illusion of control, trying to light your own torch?

God might be calling you to loosen your grip on the familiar and embrace a path that calls for faith over sight.

He invites you to fix your eyes on Him, trusting that He knows the way through every valley and up every mountain. And while those mountaintops might inspire you, it's the uncharted territory that shapes your character for the rest of the journey.

Let the gentle glow of His Word be your constant companion. Though the path ahead may feel uncertain, rest assured that God is both the light and the guide.

Each step in faith shapes you into who He's called you to be—rooted in His truth, strengthened by His love, and prepared for the plans He has designed specifically for you. Do not settle for the compromise of the comfortable. You no longer need the floodlight of certainty; the lamp of His presence is enough.

ENTRUSTED

PRAYER:

Heavenly Father, thank You for being my guide and shining light on my path when I cannot see the way forward. I ask You to unsettle me—to pull me out of the comfort zones that keep me from experiencing Your fullness. Lead me, even when I'm tempted to stay where it's safe. Help me to surrender my need to know the entire journey. Give me faith to trust You with the unknown and courage to take the next right step where Your light leads. In Jesus' name, Amen.

DAY TWENTY-NINE

FROM SCARCITY TO ABUNDANCE

> **SCRIPTURE:**
>
> *Look at the birds of the air; they do not sow or reap or store away in barns, and yet your heavenly Father feeds them. Are you not much more valuable than they? Can any one of you by worrying add a single hour to your life?*
>
> *And why do you worry about clothes? See how the flowers of the field grow. They do not labor or spin. Yet I tell you that not even Solomon in all his splendor was dressed like one of these.*
> —Matthew 6:26-29

I used to think peace was a math problem. A certain balance in the bank. A savings account that made me feel safe. A plan so airtight that I could exhale without fear of the unknown. I thought I could calculate my way to peace.

But somehow, no matter how much I saved or how carefully I forecasted, the finish line of "enough" kept moving. It was like chasing a mirage—always shifting, always just out of reach. I kept thinking, *Just a little more, then I'll be safe.*

We want God to give us 'decade bread'—enough provision to secure our future for the next ten years. But He teaches us to pray for *'daily bread.'* He gives us enough for today so that we have to come back to Him for tomorrow's portion.

Can you relate? Maybe for you, it's not actually about the money. Maybe it's the need to control an outcome. Maybe you've bought into the lie that if you hustle harder, push further, and grip tighter, you can finally secure your own future. We convince ourselves that if we can build a big enough safety net, we won't need to depend on anyone else.

But God never designed our souls to find security in what we store up. He didn't call us to hoard resources; He called us to trust Him.

"Look at the birds of the air," He whispers to the saver. *"They don't have barns or bank accounts, yet I provide for them."*

Notice He didn't say the birds don't fly, or hunt, or work. They do. But they don't *worry*. They don't stockpile out of fear that the Father might forget them tomorrow.

"Consider the flowers of the field," He reminds the spender. *"They don't accumulate, yet they're clothed in more beauty than Solomon himself."*

God's definition of abundance has nothing to do with the size of your portfolio and everything to do with the posture of your heart.

When we operate out of a scarcity mindset, we start to believe the world's frantic whisper: There isn't enough. You have to fight for your share. We cling. We negotiate out of fear. We hustle for our worth.

But God's heart for us is so much kinder than that.

He invites us to operate from a place of deep, settled trust—knowing that He has already gone ahead of us. He isn't panicking over your cash flow. He isn't surprised by your needs.

I'm learning that the most powerful prayer I can pray isn't for more money or more certainty—it's for more wisdom.

Why? Because money solves a problem for a moment, but wisdom changes your trajectory for a lifetime. Money is simply a resource; wisdom is the divine strategy to steward it. If we have abundance but lack wisdom, we will squander the blessing. If we have certainty but lack wisdom, we will become complacent. But if we have wisdom, we can navigate any season—feast or famine—with a steady hand.

Money is simply a resource; wisdom is the divine strategy to steward it.

So that is my request. I am praying for the wisdom to trust Him. Wisdom to release my grip on the outcome. Wisdom to see that my security isn't in what I can hold, but in Who holds me.

Because here's the truth: Every single time, He has provided. Every single time, He has been faithful. And He will be faithful again.

If you are in a season where the numbers aren't adding up, and fear is asking, *What if God doesn't come through?* let's flip the script. Let's stop asking, *Will He provide?* and start declaring, *He is my Source.*

When we make that shift, we stop clinging and start giving. We stop striving and start trusting.

God's provision was never meant to be stockpiled; it was meant to be deployed through us. So today, instead of gripping your assets tightly, open your hands. Instead of fearing the lack, let's trust His abundance. And instead of striving for more, let's rest in the "enough" He has already given.

PRAYER:

Lord, I surrender my fears about provision to You. Help me to trust that You are my Source—not my work, not my bank account, but You alone. Shift my heart from scarcity to abundance, from striving to rest. Teach me to steward what You've given me with wisdom and generosity, knowing that Your provision is always enough. In Jesus' name, Amen.

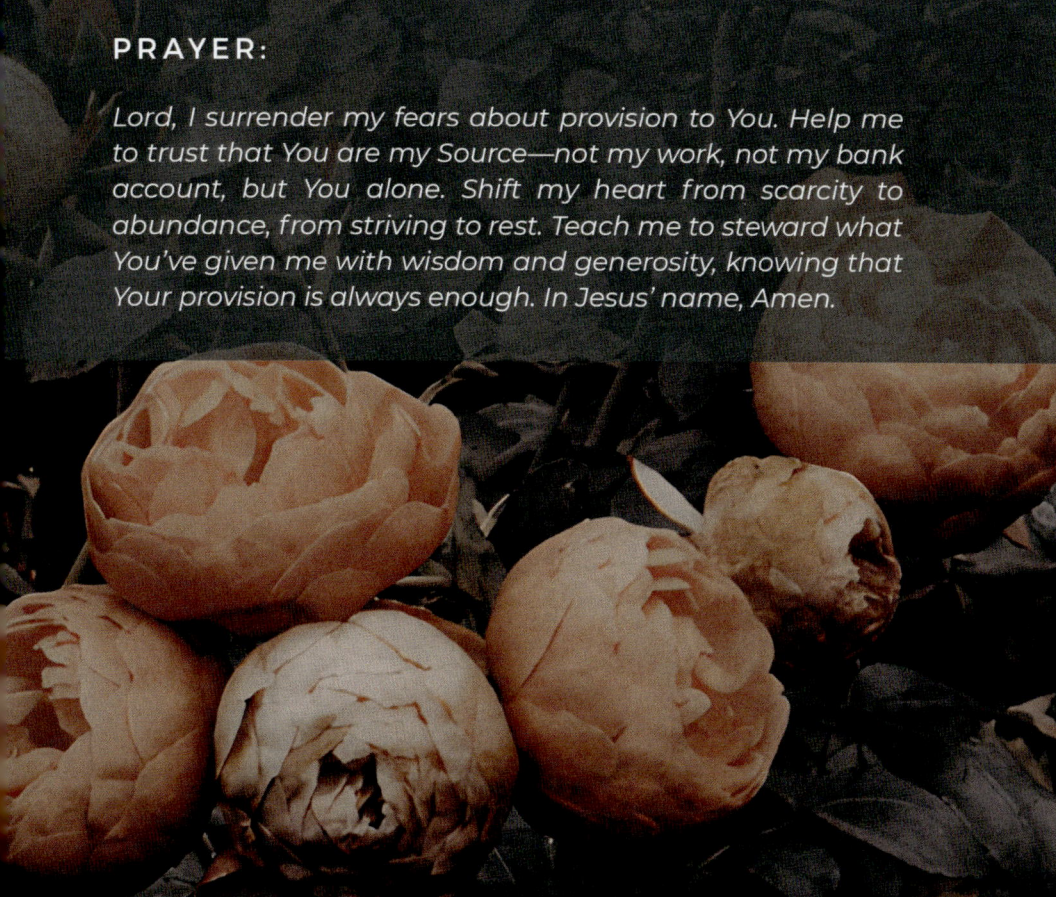

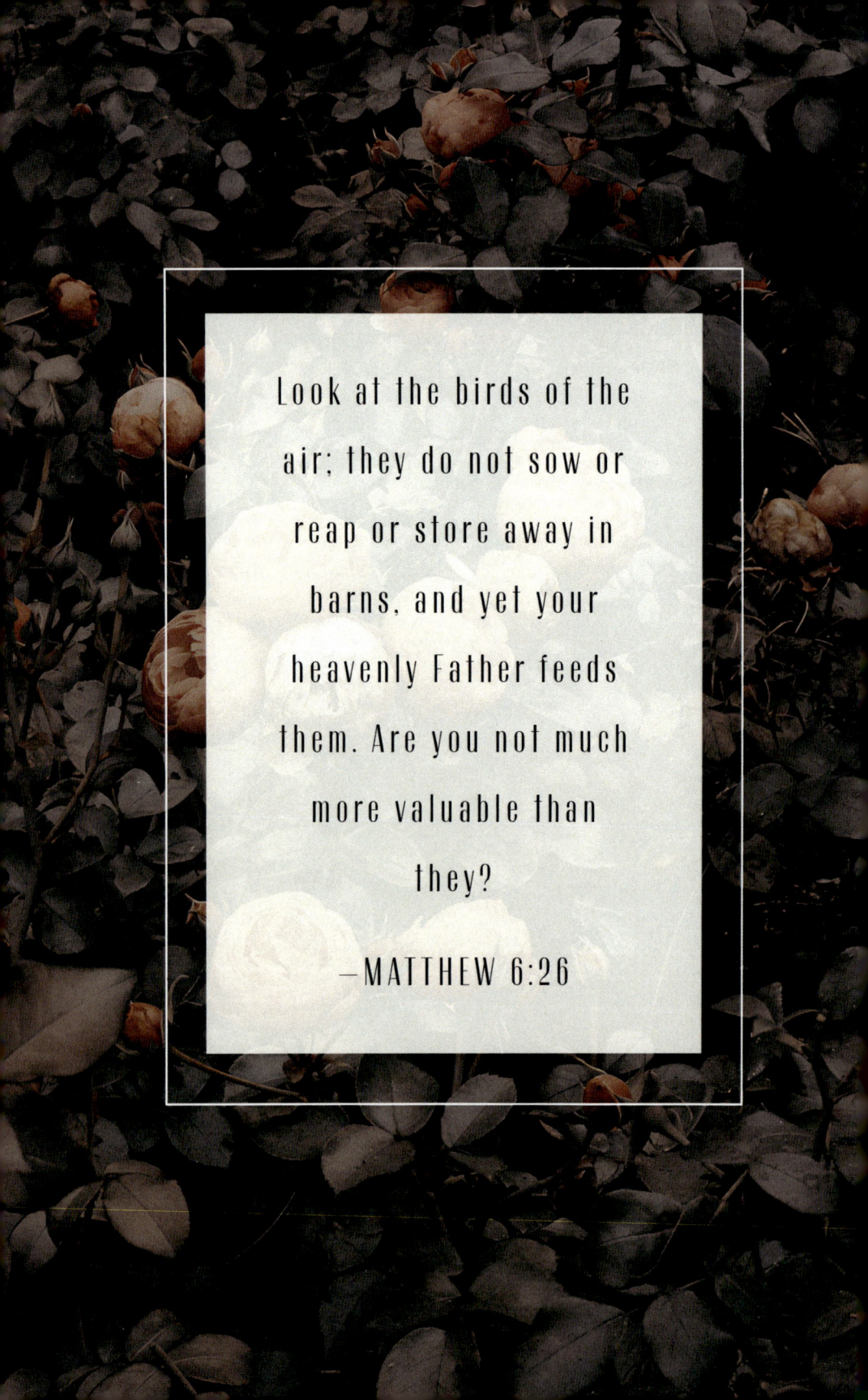

> Look at the birds of the air; they do not sow or reap or store away in barns, and yet your heavenly Father feeds them. Are you not much more valuable than they?
>
> —MATTHEW 6:26

DAY THIRTY

ENLARGE MY TERRITORY

SCRIPTURE:

Jabez cried out to the God of Israel, 'Oh, that you would bless me and enlarge my territory! Let your hand be with me, and keep me from harm so that I will be free from pain.' And God granted his request. —1 Chronicles 4:10

Have you ever wondered if it's okay to ask God to bless your business, your career, or your goals?

The answer is a resounding *yes!*

The prayer of Jabez reminds us that God's blessings reach every area of our lives, including our professional pursuits.

Jabez didn't just ask God for help—he boldly invited Him into the very center of his life and work, recognizing that only God could be the foundation of his success.

Maybe you're worn out from chasing goals that don't deliver. Maybe you feel stuck, striving for impact only to continue spinning in circles. So often, when it comes to our passions and pursuits, we find ourselves teetering back and forth between self-reliance and surrender.

The world urges us to go after "more" on our own terms, yet the more we pursue success without God, the emptier it feels.

As leaders longing to use our influence for His glory, the very first place to search for God's best is on our knees—inviting Him into every detail of our lives.

As leaders longing to use our influence for His glory, the very first place to search for God's best is on our knees—inviting Him into every detail of our lives.

SEEKING BLESSINGS

Picture yourself starting each day with a small but powerful prayer like that of Jabez—*"Oh, that you would bless me."* This alone opens us to receive His goodness, wisdom, and grace—all essential for fulfilling our calling.

If you've ever hesitated to bring your deepest desires before God because it feels selfish, pause and remember this: Your longings don't scare God. When we approach Him with humble hearts, fully surrendered to His will, we can ask *boldly*—not because we're entitled, but because *He invites us to*. Asking is an act of trust in the One who knows what we need better than we do.

In Genesis 32:26, Jacob was bold enough to wrestle with God and even refused to let go until he was blessed.

We are encouraged to come boldly to the throne of grace. The Lord invites us to ask with confidence (Hebrews 4:16) for the things that align with His will and Kingdom's purposes.

Imagine the resources, the strength, and the vision we receive when we invite Him in. God wants to bless us, to go before us, and help us dream beyond our own reach.

Jabez's prayer was bold—he dared to ask God for blessings beyond what he could see. Yet how often do we stop short, believing we should keep our passion small? Instead, let's approach God with full confidence, remembering we are His children and that we have access to a Father who desires to bless us, especially when we are in alignment with Him.

EXPANDING INFLUENCE

Building on Jabez's bold request, his next prayer—*"that You would enlarge my territory"*—was a desire for influence.

While we often connect *territory* with land or wealth, for the Kingdom leader, territory is about capacity. Jabez's heart was set on having a wider reach—more opportunities to serve God.

Imagine praying for God to increase your influence—more ways to serve, witness, and spread light where it's needed most.

Embracing a call to greater influence often takes us out of our comfort zone and into uncharted territory. God calls us to step beyond the familiar, knowing that true growth requires deep trust.

To ask God to enlarge our territory is to invite Him to stretch our capacity for stewardship. It is a dangerous, beautiful prayer that says, *'Lord, do not let my human limitations define Your Kingdom impact.'* He answers not just by giving us more ground, but by giving us the spiritual grit to hold it.

When we pray this, we aren't just asking for success; we are asking for the holy responsibility of carrying His light into rooms we couldn't enter on our own.

To ask God to enlarge our territory is to invite Him to stretch our capacity for stewardship. It is a dangerous, beautiful prayer that says, 'Lord, do not let my human limitations define Your Kingdom impact.'

RELYING ON GOD'S PRESENCE

As Jabez continued his prayer, *"Let Your hand be with me,"* he acknowledged the necessity of God's presence to guide him.

He understood that a larger influence requires God's hand to sustain it.

In a world that praises self-made success and independence, God's way calls us to be *Spirit-led* and *God-dependent*. The paths He opens for us may look unconventional to the marketplace. Yet, if we're willing to follow His lead, He will take us where we could never go alone.

In a world that praises self-made success and independence, God's way calls us to be Spirit-led and God-dependent.

When you step into the unknown, others may question your strategy. But no opinion can outweigh the purpose God has spoken over your life. Every gift you've been given and every unique calling you carry was designed by Him to bear fruit for His Kingdom. True success is measured by what His hand sustains.

REQUESTING PROTECTION

Lastly, Jabez prayed, *"Keep me from evil so that I will be free from pain."*

With success often comes new challenges. Jabez understood that greater influence could expose him to dangers and temptations that might hinder his calling. He didn't want his impact to come at the cost of his integrity or peace.

His prayer reminds us to stay close to God, asking for covering and discernment as we step into new territory.

This plea for protection wasn't random. In fact, it was deeply personal. The name *Jabez* means "born out of pain." His very identity carried the reminder of hardship. But his prayer reached for hope—a desire to rise above the circumstances of his origin. He was asking God to redefine his story, moving it from pain to promise.

We, too, can ask God to shape our lives according to His promises—transforming our past into a testimony for His glory. The prayer of Jabez reminds us we can boldly ask God for more—more impact, more blessing, and more influence for His Kingdom.

ENLARGE MY TERRITORY

This isn't about chasing self-gain; it's about recognizing the beautiful truth that we have *one* life to pour out for God's glory.

Are we courageous enough to ask Him for something so big, so beyond our resources, that only He could make it happen?

Let's approach Him with open hearts, ready to be vessels for His work. When we place our trust in Him, there's no limit to the Kingdom-sized things He can do in and through us.

PRAYER:

Heavenly Father, open my eyes to see beyond my present circumstances and help me envision the possibilities You have for me. I trust in Your hand to guide and sustain me as I step into the opportunities You set before me. Bless me and enlarge my territory, Lord, that I may serve You with greater impact and bring glory to Your name. Protect me from harm and guard my heart, so that my influence always reflects Your character. May everything I do point others to You. In Jesus' name, Amen.

NOTES

1. Bible Hub: Search, Read, Study the Bible in Many Languages, "Strong's Hebrew: *Avodah* – 5656," *Bible Hub*, accessed June 28, 2025, Strong's Hebrew: 5656. עֲבֹדָה (abodah) — Service, labor, work, worship. https://biblehub.com/strongs/hebrew/5656.htm

2. Bible Hub: Search, Read, Study the Bible in Many Languages, "Strong's Hebrew: *Qavah* – 6960," *Bible Hub*, accessed June 28, 2025, Strong's Hebrew: 6960. קָוָה (qavah) — To wait, to look for, to hope, to expect. https://biblehub.com/strongs/hebrew/6960.htm

3. Bible Hub: Search, Read, Study the Bible in Many Languages, "Strong's Hebrew: *Niyr* – 5216," *Bible Hub*, accessed June 28, 2025, Strong's Hebrew: 5216. נֵר (ner) — Lamp, light. https://biblehub.com/strongs/hebrew/5216.htm

NICE TO MEET YOU!

Jen Marrufo is a writer, worship leader, and creative visionary. She writes with the conviction that words anchored in truth are the seeds of a legacy that far outlasts a lifetime. With a degree in Christian Ministry and Psychology from Ozark Christian College, she enjoys helping others process their story, grow in their faith, see their potential, and experience the redemptive power of Jesus.

She writes from the rolling hills of southwest Missouri, where she lives with her husband and two children—who keep her inspired, grounded, and often very caffeinated. When she's not raising tiny humans, she's thinking up her next idea, creating freely, or scribbling ideas on anything with a blank space.

Her writing spans devotionals, children's books, and honest reflections on trauma, healing, identity, and the call of God. She has a heart for the lost and all who want to make a difference for the Kingdom and simply need a little nudge to believe they still can.

Connect on social to see behind-the-scenes content and learn more about upcoming projects.

Thank You for Reading!

Your time and attention mean the world to me. I'd love to hear what resonated with you, what surprised you, or even what you'd like to see more of in the future.

If you found this book meaningful, would you take two minutes to leave a review on Amazon? Your feedback not only helps me grow as a writer—it also helps other readers find the message of hope and purpose within these pages.

Thank you so much for your support.

This is just the beginning.

jen

A PERSONAL INVITATION

New friend, we've walked through a lot of pages together. We've looked at the hard parts of life and the hope we're desperately trying to cling to. But I would be missing the most important part of this journey if I didn't ask you a simple, yet life-altering question: *Do you know the One who holds it all together?*

For years, I tried to manage my own life. I tried to arrange the pieces perfectly, hoping that if I tried hard enough, the ache in my soul would settle. But the truth is, no amount of striving, planning, or achieving can fill the space in our hearts that was made for Jesus. We don't need to be perfect to come to Him; we need to be willing to surrender our brokenness to His wholeness.

Jesus isn't waiting for you to clean up your act. He's standing at the door of your heart right now, ready to trade your heaviness for His peace. He died on the cross so that our mistakes, our sins, and our separation from God wouldn't have the final say. He rose from the grave to prove that new beginnings are possible—even for you. Even right now.

If you feel a tug in your spirit, that's Him. That is the gentle whisper of God inviting you home. You don't need fancy words. You simply need an honest heart. You can pray something like this:

PRAYER:

I come to You today honestly acknowledging that I need You. I have tried to navigate this life on my own, but I know that I have sinned and fallen short of Your glory. I declare this confession of truth over my life today: **I believe that Jesus is the Christ, the Son of the living God, my Lord and my Savior.** *Thank You for dying on the cross for my sins and rising from the dead to give me new life. I surrender my heart to You. Be my Lord, be my Savior, and lead me from this day forward. In Jesus' name, Amen.*

If you prayed that prayer, the heavens are celebrating, and I am cheering you on! You have just made the best decision of your life. You are not alone, you are loved, and you are His.

Made in the USA
Coppell, TX
11 March 2026